NEAR UNTO GOD

ABRAHAM KUYPER

Daily meditations
adapted for contemporary Christians by
James C. Schaap

CRC Publications
Grand Rapids, Michigan

William B. Eerdmans Publishing Company
Grand Rapids, Michigan

The Scripture quotations in this publication are from
the KING JAMES VERSION.

Near Unto God, © 1997, CRC Publications, 2850
Kalamazoo Avenue SE, Grand Rapids, MI 49560.

Cover: Images ©1996 PhotoDisc, Inc.

ISBN 1-56212-254-1

Library of Congress Cataloging-in-Publication Data
Kuyper, Abraham, 1837-1920.
    [Nabij God te zijn. English]
    Near unto God / Abraham Kuyper.
        p.   cm.
    "Daily meditations adapted for contemporary
Christians by James C. Schaap."
    ISBN 1-56212-254-1
    1. Meditations. 2. Devotional calendars—
Reformed Church. 3. Christian life—Reformed
(Reformed Church) authors. I. Schaap, James C.,
1948-   . II. Title
BV4832.2.K8413   1997
242—dc21   97-7877
                                                      CIP

10 9 8 7 6 5 4 3 2 1

NEAR UNTO GOD

ABRAHAM KUYPER

Daily meditations
adapted for contemporary Christians by
James C. Schaap

As I worked through these meditations, it soon became apparent to me that a significant number were based upon specific biblical language occurring only in the KJV. For that reason, this book uses Scripture texts as they appear in the English King James Version of the Holy Bible.

—JCS

Preface

The appearance of a new edition of something written by Abraham Kuyper is always for me a noteworthy event. But I am especially pleased about the publication of this volume. I first discovered these meditations at a point in my life when I thought I needed to take a break from being a "Kuyperian." These profound reflections on biblical materials assured me that Kuyper had experienced the same need in his own life.

Before I read these meditations, I had come to think of Kuyper as a key mentor in my attempts to understand the proper contours of Christian activism. In my reaction against the kind of position that scorned any kind of active Christian involvement in efforts at social and political reform, I had gotten much inspiration from Kuyper's writings. His 1898 Princeton lectures on Calvinism as a "world and life view"—which I read and reread—were especially helpful, as was his *Christianity and the Class Struggle*. In my own teaching and writing on social topics I was fond of quoting the manifesto that Kuyper issued at the end of his great "Sphere Sovereignty" address: 'There is not one square inch of the entire creation about which Jesus Christ does not cry out, 'This is mine! This belongs to me!' "

But claiming all of those square inches for the kingdom of Jesus Christ can leave one breathless. So there came a time when I decided to concentrate again on cultivating some personal spiritual resources—not as a return to an anti-activist pietism, but simply out of a recognition that the

Christian life cannot be sustained by activism alone. So I began to search out the spiritual classics. And in doing so I discovered that Kuyper himself had written the kind of meditations on biblical themes that could feed the weary soul. This Christian activist—political leader, prodigious journalist, educational reformer, theological warrior—also felt the need at frequent intervals in his life to write out his thoughts about what it means for the individual believer to turn away from the demands of the active life and retreat into that very private, sacred space where the soul is alone with her Maker. And he did so in a very wedded piety with intellectual integrity and a passion for justice.

I have often wished that these meditations were available to a large audience in North America. The past decade or so has seen a heightened awareness of the importance of "spirituality." Writings about prayer, contemplation, and the various spiritual disciplines have been produced on a large scale. And I have benefited greatly from what someone has lightheartedly described as "the spirituality bust." My own shelves hold muchread volumes by the likes of the Desert Fathers, Thomas a Kempis, Theresa of Lisieux, and Henri Nouwen. I keep coming back to Kuyper, however, because he too offers unique—and I must add with a sense of passion, uniquely Reformed—insights into the life of the spirit. Kuyper's spiritual writings deserve a prominent place on the shelf of Christian classics, but not just because they are worthy of scholarly attention from those who map out the varieties of Christian spirituality. I want others to take delight, as I have, in Kuyper's profound insights into what it means to live, as he loved to put it, *coram deo,* before the face of God.

Kuyper wrote in a specific cultural context in nineteenth-century Holland. In this marvelous volume, James Schaap has updated his writings, giving him a fresh voice that speaks to very contemporary challenges and opportunities. I am confident that these meditations will touch the deep places in the souls of many Christians who want to know more about what it means to be integrated persons who live their lives "near unto God."

—Richard J. Mouw

Introduction

I am not a fatalist or a determinist, and I don't have much faith in those who argue that our identities are entirely prescribed by the DNA particles that make our fingerprints unique or determine the length of our toes. Even so, about some bits and pieces of who we are, I'm afraid we don't have much choice.

I am, for better or for worse, someone shaped by the work of a portly historical figure named Abraham Kuyper, a former prime minister of the Netherlands, a noted clergyman and theologian, and a prolific journalist, about whom I know very little more than I've just related. I've never studied Kuyper's theology, read his political treatises, or paged through much more than a chapter or two from his biography. What I know is that he was, and still is, central to the ethos in which I was raised and within which I continue to work. That ethos is the precious heritage of a diminutive American immigrant subculture, the Dutch Reformed, a group of folks long ago forgotten by their contemporary European siblings and slowly now disappearing, as all ethnic subcultures do, within the stew constantly brewing in the American melting pot.

This man Kuyper is an intimate of mine, even though I never met him. Somewhere inside me he holds sway with much more authority than, say, President Teddy Roosevelt, who would have been his contemporary and was himself Dutch-American. Kuyper's mind—his ideas and vision—are a part of me that has always been there, even when I didn't know it was.

But he doesn't haunt me. He's not a bad memory. Something of what I am I attribute to him, and I do so thankfully.

That I even know the name Abraham Kuyper may well be a legacy of the quest for identity most North Americans—Jewish, Irish Catholic, Russian Orthodox, Swedish Baptist, Norwegian Lutheran—mount at some time in their lives. My ethno-religious roots are deeply planted in nineteenth-century Dutch Calvinism, a legacy I didn't choose any more than I chose my parents or the place of my birth.

Rootedness suggests values. My own immigrant great-grandparents stuck with old-country traditions via an adherence built upon faith, even though anthropologists, I'm sure, would assert that their holding to the old ways was simply a way to maintain identity in nineteenth-century polyglot America. Part of what they held to was inscribed in their souls by this man, Abraham Kuyper. So he was part of what they passed along to me, even though, growing up, I never heard the man's name in my own family home.

For me, getting to know Abraham Kuyper is an exercise in knowing myself. If the greatest knowledge, as Socrates thought, is knowledge of self, then gaining an understanding of what we've come from is no mean accomplishment. Willa Cather once said that every major theme a writer considers is something planted within the soul long before adulthood. If that's true, then for me, knowing something about Kuyper helps me visualize more clearly what I've been considering for most of my life and two decades of writing—and why.

What I'm suggesting by all of this is why I wrote this book. There is a history in my interest, and it is part of the story, part of that same Kuyper's legacy. A few years ago, *The Banner*, the denominational magazine of the Christian Reformed Church in North America, asked several of its members to list the books they love. Richard Mouw, President of Fuller Seminary in California, named *To Be Near Unto God* as his favorite nonfiction book, saying, "Kuyper is one of my heroes, and these meditations are a regular source of spiritual nourishment for me."

That recommendation sent me to our old, oak bookcases, the ones that hold what I have of my grandfather's library, as well as that of his father-in-law, my great-grandfather. My grandfather was John C. Schaap, a preacher in the Christian Reformed Church; and his wife, Nelle Hemkes Schaap, was the daughter of Gerrit Klaas Hemkes, a professor at the school that has since become Calvin College and Seminary, Grand Rapids, Michigan.

From one of them—probably my grandfather—I inherited *To Be Near Unto God*, a volume of Kuyper's meditations of almost a century ago, in an English translation by John De Vries. It is an Eerdmans publication dated 1918, the year both my father and mother were born.

The copy I own is a tattered, little, brown book, small enough to fit in your hand, but thick as a Bible. It has many underlined and bracketed passages. Some of the pages look as if they've been folded back for quick and ready access. The binding is torn, but only a few pages are loose. It looks used, very much so.

However, even before I picked it out of the old books in our library and even before I read Mouw's recommendation, I knew something about that book. I knew it contained a more risky Abraham Kuyper than the powerful imminence my own immigrant tradition remembers. I recall hearing people say that the Kuyper of *To Be Near Unto God* was a highly "spiritual" Kuyper, someone whose religious enthusiasms made at least some of his twentieth-century disciples somewhat anxious.

Let me stop here for a moment to explain something of the Kuyper legacy as I've come to know it and as I actively pass it along to my students. Christianity bestows on its adherents a double identity: we are citizens of both this world and the next, a reality that often creates an identity crisis and some confusion of purpose. First of all, we are, as recipients of grace, inheritors of a spiritual kingdom, the world to come in eternity. "This world is not my home; I'm just a passin' through," claims the old hymn. Whenever eternal peace is compared with the turbulent listing of our lives on earth, placid heavenly waters seem especially inviting.

But as long as we live here on earth, we are citizens of this world—not simply heaven-gazers. To look only toward heaven means looking past the world God tells us he loved so breathtakingly much (John 3:16). Total investment in the life hereafter, some contemporary Kuyper followers might say, means shirking the responsibilities and joys of the world God lovingly sets us within.

What we live with is not so much a paradox as a pair of mutually exclusive demands on our time and interests. It's very simple for Christians to fall off the tightrope created by Christ's injunction about "in and not of." On the one side, some fall toward what some believers still call worldliness, while on the other, some fall into otherworldliness. Balance is both difficult and demanding. Our job is to look to glory without overlooking God's world. That's not easy.

What I've always believed about Kuyper is that he sensibly walked the line between our spiritual and earthly concerns. Even in his life, one can't miss the balance. He was both preacher and prime minister, both theologian and politician, both writer of meditations and social theorist. Those who know his personal life better than I do may well call me a victim of his mythos, but the Kuyper who has given me a paradigm by which to see my own calling is a Kuyper who was, at once, both near unto God and near unto God's world.

In fact, I believe it was Kuyper's ability to balance the claims of a Christian's inherent double identity that, at least on this side of the Atlantic, made his name into an adjective I'd used respectfully time and time again—Kuyperian—even though I had never read a word of his work. With that adjective, the institution where I teach often defines its mission, with equal doses of the respect and admiration we might give the word Calvinistic.

But I also knew that this little devotional book, *To Be Near Unto God*, would offer me an Abraham Kuyper who occasionally embarrasses his followers, a Kuyper whose meditative soliloquies flirt with a spirituality so akin to ecstasy that it brought furrows to the brows of the more stolid Dutch ancestors. But don't misunderstand. That furrow was not simply the result of violated sensibilities, the effect of a Puritan who suddenly stands up in the meeting house and sounds off to his peers in glossalia. What made Kuyperians anxious about *To Be Near Unto God*, I knew, was the riskiness of Kuyper's spirituality. Quite simply, the book was potentially dangerous, not to his image but to his followers. They might, on reading it, become so caught up in his quest for what we've come to call *spirituality*, one's personal relationship to God, that they would renege on their commitment to the world. This Kuyper, by reputation, maybe went a bit too far.

So I had several reasons to read my grandfather's old John De Vries translation. First, Richard Mouw recommended it; I respect him. Second, my own ancestors read it faithfully; I wanted to know them—and myself—better. Third, some people considered the book a bit chancy; I've always liked controversial books. Finally, I'd never before read a word of a man whose mind in many ways shaped me deeply.

I started reading with no thought of writing anything. I'd just finished a novel, and I thought my grandfather's book would make an interesting daily devotional. I started reading, knowing that what I was going to discover was something already vaguely within me. Call it self-discovery, sentimentality, or nostalgia. It was all of that.

I loved what I read. I found myself in a mind worth knowing well. I was impressed, not only with the range Kuyper must have had over both this life and the next, but also with the nature of the deep spirituality that drives the book. Our whole purpose here, the purpose of life, Kuyper would say, is, first and foremost, "to be near unto God."

I read six or seven meditations and decided to keep a journal. I've never had a particularly sticky mind. If I want to remember what I read, I take notes, either in the margins or in a notebook. So I started with notes to myself, pulling what I thought was the essential Kuyper from sentences translated in a prose style probably typical of the turn of the century, but exhausting, even aggravating, today. John De Vries likely intended to make Kuyper sound like a turn-of-the-century learned Princeton divine. But simply reading the sentences demanded substantial pruning and cutting, even slashing, to get at Kuyper. Redoing sentences was something I had to do if I wanted to understand.

That process made me think it might be enjoyable to cut the meditations down to their heart. So I started editing as an exercise, a writer's aerobics.

I'd done maybe a half dozen when I realized that Kuyper's meditations in *To Be Near Unto God* needed badly to be freed from prose as exaggerated as the wings on an old Chrysler. What this man Kuyper has to say is simply too good to be petrified.

What you have in your hands is the book that resulted. That's how I came to write—or rewrite—this book. It was a wonderful experience.

What did I learn? A number of things. First, those who claim that inheritors of a Reformed or Calvinist worldview have no tradition of piety are, at best, uninformed. No one can read this book and come away believing such nonsense. Kuyper's spirituality is a witness, a century after the devotions were penned.

But I also learned that Kuyper's expression of spirituality is a world away from contemporary public demonstrations of piousness. For him, to be near unto God is something private, quiet, and deep—what he calls the "hidden walk." From the outside, and in the pew, the countenance Kuyper wants to create may very well appear cold. It may seem to lack drama or a heavy bass. But it isn't at all cold. Read him yourself. You'll see.

Some things that I learned didn't surprise me. Look at the way he uses science in, for instance, "Hearken Unto Me." Kuyper was not afraid of life, of technological change; he seems to have been driven to locate his God in every inch of his creation.

But I was surprised to find him so tolerant, exhorting his readers in several meditations to allow for individual differences in both coming to God and in expressing individual faith (see "O God, My God," for example). What impressed me about that tolerance was his understanding of human nature—how easy it is for us, having come to God ourselves, to prescribe the means by which others should.

For me at least, the greatest discovered joy in reading a nearly century-old book of meditations was Kuyper's vivid exposition of the attributes of God. Let me try to explain. Preaching, like writing meditations, becomes Sunday-schoolish when the word *should* is too liberally sprinkled about. I believe an old rule of thumb for writing extends to preaching as well: "Show, don't tell." Convincing writing always pictures, never points; always demonstrates, never demands. Kuyper describes God and his love so thoughtfully and so caringly that our response to what he says is not so much directed as discipled by the reality he pictures. Kuyper doesn't need to tell us how to be spiritual because in so many of the meditations he shows us, beautifully, by describing God with intimate respect and awe.

But I've gone on too long. You have the book in your hand. Read it for yourself, for there are much better reasons than nostalgia to read Abraham Kuyper's meditations, a greater goal than a search for identity. The best motivation remains its title: *Near Unto God.* The book may well be one hundred years old, but aside from a few paragraphs about thee and thou and a reference to outdoor plumbing, very little substance needed to be cut. It is, to me, a devotional classic.

Kuyper honored ordinary people; that's evident in the book. The De Vries translation may well have been wonderful for my grandfather, but a contemporary reader will find much of it almost inaccessible because of the prose style. I've tried to deliver the essential Kuyper to the ordinary people he respected. This may be wishful thinking, but something in me says that were Kuyper alive today, he'd approve of this abridgment.

Finally, a story I've waited too long to tell. Henrietta Ten Harmsel, emeritus professor of English at Calvin College, told me that when her father was dying, she used to read to him, daily, passages from Abraham Kuyper. Her father, Anton Ten Harmsel, lived and died a long way from Amsterdam, the Netherlands. He immigrated from Holland and came to the same region of North America where I now live, Iowa, a place most notable for corn and beans and hogs—and back then, other immigrant farmers. Here in Iowa he farmed in a number of places and was a devoted

Christian and avid reader, who with his wife raised their children and led an active life in the community's church and school.

Professor Ten Harmsel read her father his daily dose of Kuyper. But one day the literature professor in her plotted a good diversion. Instead of *To Be Near Unto God*, she pulled out a John Donne meditation on Peter's denial of Christ, which contains the repeated refrain, "Has the cock crowed for you?" She read her father this homily from the famous Anglican preacher and poet.

When she was through, her father nodded his head, barely raising it from the pillow, then looked up at his daughter and said, in the Dutch language, *"Net zowat zo goed als Abraham Kuyper,"* which is to say, "Almost as good as Abraham Kuyper."

There's something in that story, just as there is in my grandfather's tattered copy of *To Be Near Unto God*, that makes me believe these Kuyper meditations are worth keeping fresh for another century of God's people, no matter what ethnic baggage those Christians haul along on their emigration to glory. In a way, identity was what I was looking for, but a wholly different identity was what I found.

Throughout, I may have altered his wardrobe, but I tried not to change the man. It is my prayer that God's nearness, the stated goal of this book's meditations, will still be its gift to new generations of believers.

James C. Schaap
Sioux Center, Iowa
October, 1996

To Be
Near Unto God

But it is good for me to be near unto God.
—Psalm 73:28

(translation from the Dutch version)

We can hold high admiration and deep respect for our nation, for nature, for beauty, for art, for the suffering of others, even for humanity itself. We can have a love for what is honest and pure, for what is good, for our heritage, our theology, our creeds.

We can even *have* a love for God, since all good that inspires love is from God, and God himself is the highest good. But when the psalmist says, "I love God," he implies something different from deep admiration and respect. What he is talking about is something intimate and personal, a relationship that makes the Good Shepherd, *our* shepherd; the Father, *our* source of life and happiness; the Covenant God, the one with whom *we* share an eternal and blessed agreement. Then, he is near.

When we know God Almighty as a presence on the paths of our lives, when we have entered into a personal, particular relationship with him, then and only then does he become *our* Father in heaven.

What we're talking about here is a relationship so personal and intimate that it can't be described in words. If you don't understand, you don't *know* God at that level. But if you deeply desire to know him in that way, then you're already on the right track.

When we know him as our personal Savior, then we have come to him and he has come to us—because the action moves in two directions. We need to seek his nearness, but he needs to come to us intimately. When he does—and when we do—what we feel is nothing less than eternal joy.

We can spend much of our lives without that closeness, sometimes desolate and forsaken. But if we know God's nearness, we know that in those moments of alienation nothing is so desirable as his return. What we seek, we find only in our return—he is near once again. Those moments, beyond description, are the great moments of our lives.

To shut ourselves up away from life in an attempt to live more fully in those moments doesn't guarantee his nearness. The darkness so characteristic of this world is, after all, a commodity we carry with us into our seclusion. We cannot hide from the weaknesses in our own hearts.

Seclusion can, however, hide us from many of the world's problems; that's why the appeal of monastic living is so strong, even if it's misguided. To run away and hide, even for purposes of seeking God, is to flee from our calling and task. Where there is no conflict, there can be no victory.

What every martyr's story makes clear is that our drawing near to God yields its sweetest blessing when, in the face of sin and the world, we know that God is beside us. That's eternal comfort. When the fig tree does not blossom and the vine will yield no fruit, then, with Habakkuk, to rejoice in God is the grandest moment of his blessed nearness.

Today, in the public square, faith is frequently shunned. Many people think belief in God is barbaric, a remnant silliness of the dark ages. There may have been a time when belief could more easily prosper in the marketplace, but in today's world faith is scorned.

Such a world is an impediment to God's nearness, to say the least. But don't throw in the towel; we know very well God hasn't. In his eternal compassion, he will come nearer and hold us up in the onslaught of a world that laughs him to shame.

The modern age is extremely dangerous to us—and even more so to our children. But he is here, as he always has been, awaiting our desire for a secret fellowship with him that will sustain us no matter what happens in our world.

To know that, to seek him passionately, and to find him, face to face, in the muddle of our travail here on earth—all of that makes us testify with the psalmist, "I love you, Lord."

THE SOULS WHICH
I HAVE MADE

For I will not contend for ever,
neither will I be always wroth:
for the spirit should fail before me,
and the souls which I have made.
—Isaiah 57:16

Anyone who writes knows the particular pleasure of seeing his or her name at the top of a story or on the spine of a book. Those who don't write may think of that pleasure as egotism or pride, but that's not necessarily so. Mrs. Smith realizes her three-year-old needs a new bed, but rather than pick one out from a store, she decides that, like her father, she would rather build it with her hands. She does. No matter what that bed looks like when it's completed, Mrs. Smith will forever look upon her handiwork with more regard than the bunks she may have bought from a catalog. What we make with our hands, we regard with very special care.

The mother who runs a daycare center in her home may have six or seven children she loves immensely, caring for them all day long, attending their hurts and their joys. But one of those children is special for no other reason than that one is hers.

The blessings that come to us as a result of our being created by the Father are beyond our comprehension. Because God fashioned us fully and completely, something within us has him in it. We have something of his power, his thought, and his creative genius, characteristics that exist in no other creature made by his hands. What's more, when we're massed together, we become the whole display of his creative power, his work of art in myriad shapes and colors and sizes. We are his masterpiece.

When any single part of that canvas is lost, the entirety of the work suffers, for God himself cannot do without any single one of us. What Jesus described in the beautiful parables of the prodigal son, the lost coin, and the lost sheep is an idea borne from the very character of God. We are all precious pieces in his collection—all of us. He cannot let go of any single part of the work of his hands.

To know God's longing for us in that way is to begin to understand God's grief at our sin.

Consider this. The director of an art museum comes to work one morning and discovers that, sometime in the night, the paintings on exhibition have been vandalized, slashed, and butchered by some madman wielding a razor blade. The director's heart nearly breaks. But then imagine the artist himself, who is called in to witness what has happened to his work. Can you imagine his horror at the travesty done to the vision he's brought to life?

Since we are the art God has created, imagine his horror at our individual sin. Even worse, imagine the scorching anger he must hold toward those who slash and butcher others by their faithlessness, those who wound the likeness of God in any of his children.

To know deeply that we are children of God, the masterpieces of his handiwork—to know that we bear our Father's image and carry his likeness—brings to all who comprehend it a clear two-fold understanding.

First, it brings consolation and comfort. We are his, indelibly marked with his own essence. He will love us because we are his own.

Second, it brings fear and trembling. Because we are his, our sin is not simply our own but a grievous wound on God's own essence.

To begin every morning of one's life with the knowledge that we have been created by God is the first step in realizing the importance of avoiding sin. God made us. Our unfaithfulness, in a ghastly way, wrenches his Father-heart.

NOT RICH TOWARDS GOD

So is he that layeth up treasure for himself,
and is not rich toward God.
—Luke 12:21

With divine clarity, Christ saw the conflict created in all of us by the love of money, even though he lived in a time when it's likely that people's needs were probably much more easily satisfied than ours are today.

Let's not be coy about it: whether we like it or not, money plays a determining role in our lives. With it, we go a long ways toward taking care of ourselves; without it, we're constantly on edge and anxious.

Making money is not inherently wrong. But while the desire to free ourselves of the problems that come with poverty should never be considered evil, to dedicate our lives to the acquisition of things makes us selfish slaves.

What the Bible calls *mammon* is really money plus Satan. Money is power in the hand. But when what's in the hand determines what's in the heart, then what's really driving us is no longer money but mammon. No man or woman can serve two masters. No one can be subject to God *and* subject to mammon.

One *can* be "rich toward God" and be rich in material blessings. Those who know themselves to be God's servants understand that money serves us and the Lord. Such people are not seduced by gold and silver or beachfront condominiums.

Some people are poor in spiritual values and rich in things of the world. They may outfit their lives in splendor and good fortune, but no one knows the emptiness in their souls better than they do.

The roughest life belongs to those poor in spiritual values *and* poor economically. For them, life offers little but ever-carping care and endless vexation.

But what does it mean, exactly, to be "rich toward God"?

Imagine everything you own blown away by a tornado—everything, even family. Nothing remains. Really, that's where each of us is at death. As we face our Maker, our real fortunes lie only in our souls, and the only riches we carry belong, really, to him.

Don't lie. Ask yourself whether anything in you is inherently valuable— in your garage, your bank account, or even in the corners of your heart. Many of us spend our lifetimes gaining wisdom, learning an art, perfecting a skill. These things bring great joy to our days, but eternally they are of little import. Hell will be littered with creative, bright people, nimble in conversation—people who have sought none of the riches of God.

To be rich with God is to own him, to be his temple, to carry in your heart the holy and glorious one wherever you go. To be rich with God is to be refreshed continuously from the Fountain of all good inside one's very own soul. The riches God brings are infinite because they are eternal.

What the Bible speaks of frequently as our "inheritance" is an inheritance in glory, a place where we will live in palaces of everlasting light more luxurious than anything Palm Beach ever dreamed of. On that eternal strip, there will be no more sin and sorrow.

To be near unto God means understanding that what we really own comes to us both in him and through him. It is a mark of our sin to recognize how difficult it is for us to know with true conviction that our fortunes lie in the Lord and not in the things of this world—and to operate on that principle. That's what Christ understood perfectly about us. ▣

IN THE COVERT
OF THY WINGS

I will abide in thy tabernacle for ever;
I will trust in the covert of thy wings.
—Psalm 61:4

The Psalms offer Scripture's richest outpouring of devotion. They illustrate the heart's intense search for divine fellowship, the most crucial relationship of our lives. The kind of true communion described in these songs, a relationship desperately desired by believers, can't be defined simply as a tie that binds us to the Creator or our faith in him. True fellowship exists where the believer has a clear knowledge of God *and* the vivid assurance that God knows him or her intimately.

"The secret of the LORD is with them that fear him; and he will show them his covenant" (Ps. 25:14). That secret we define as a *conviction*, a radical turning to God, a wonderful union with him.

Although that union has no parallels in the rest of our lives, God has given us other intimate relationships to help us define true fellowship with him. Old friends get together, and joy overflows as all pretense falls. Wives and husbands know each other to the depths. Parents discern their children in deep and abiding ways. These intimate human relationships are helpful, but they are only approximations of true fellowship with God, of the relationship the Old Testament saints knew when they "walked with God." No human being can *dwell with us* as fully as our God can. "One thing have I desired of the LORD," says David, "that I will seek after; that I may dwell in the house of the LORD all the days of my life ..." (Ps. 27:4).

The family home is the nursery of love. Intimacy grows where we live together. But in Scripture the home is always only a means to an end, the medium by which we begin to understand the relationship we have together with God. Throughout the Exodus journey, the house of the Lord, God's temple and tabernacle, was the physical manifestation of his reality. To the early Israelites, he was literally there—and because he was, he was real. It's no wonder the psalmists continuously testify to their deep desire to belong in the house of the Lord or to serve as doorkeepers where he abides.

Even though today there is no longer a centrally located temple, no physical building where God can be said to exist, we still assume that God himself has a home. "Our Father who art in heaven," we pray, after the pattern Christ gave us. God still dwells somewhere, even though the temple in time and space is long ago gone.

To seek him as if he were not here at all is to seek only a spiritual God—and he is more than an absentee landlord. "In the covert of thy wings," David says, he can live for eternity in the tabernacle of God (Ps. 61:4). What is the nature of that eternal tabernacle?

To dwell in the house of the Lord forever means that every day of our lives we know fellowship with him, that his voice sounds in our lives as regularly as the ticking of the mantle clock, that we know his presence always—no matter where, no matter what. To live under the covert of his wings is to see him at every moment. He is in our home.

To be near unto God is the sole end of humankind. Under the covert of his wings, the human soul meets the divine. In his hand is the sacred touch. Here, one perceives and experiences God, realizes that nothing, no power on earth or beneath it, no creature or perceived deity can stand between ourselves and our God. God tabernacles with us.

Actually, the imagery is scary. It can be—and sometimes is—taken too literally. No matter how intimate our relationship with him, we are not God; but we can be one with him. If we understand the difference and are on our guard, we can be wonderfully blessed by the imagery he gives us with friends and family, the intimacy of our relationships here on earth.

Only one Mediator brings us at-one with God. All of us, impure and unholy, find communion with our Creator only through his Son, Jesus Christ, the solitary means to true and abiding fellowship in the house of the Lord.

WHEN HE TURNETH HIMSELF UNTO THE PRAYER

Do not hide your face from me in the day when I am in trouble;
incline thine ear to me: in the day when I call, answer me speedily.
—Psalm 102:2

C an God—will he?—hide himself from us? Isn't it true that God
knows what's on our minds even before we bring it to him in
prayer? Doesn't the idea that he might not listen imply indifference?
Doesn't he care? Are there moments when he's simply absent without
leave? What's going on here?

What the psalmist is talking about seems to happen frequently, doesn't
it? In the middle of trouble, we come to God and ask his aid. But sometimes the trouble we face doesn't go away. At those times God seems to
take the side of, say, cancer or whatever it is that threatens. Even though
no prayers can possibly ascend from cancer cells, God can appear to be on
the side of the disease or whatever imperils us or those close to us.

"Do not hide your face from me in the day when I am in trouble; incline
your ear to me: in the day when I call, answer me speedily." This verse
helps some, because it shows us that the psalmist expects help someday.
But it also illustrates that, at least for the time being, God simply isn't in
the building.

Everything we believe about God is not only undermined but almost
destroyed by our perception of God's absence from our lives. Can he
actually be somewhere else?

What's ironic is that nobody is more sure of God's presence elsewhere
than the very psalmist who here questions the Lord's whereabouts.
"... there is not a word in my tongue," he says in Psalm 139:4, "but, lo, O

Lord, thou knowest it altogether." How can he believe in the omnipresence of God *and* his absence?

What's more, we know more than the psalmist does because we know Christ. Before Bethlehem, God spoke in words. In Christ, he made the word flesh, human. The incarnation—Immanuel—is the promise of *God with us.* The great comfort of the Christian faith is that he will not leave us abandoned, that he is forever and eternally our God because he came to us, as we are.

But there's more. We exist in his image. How can God deny or abandon that which actually holds his own form? We are his children. He loves us—doesn't he?—*because* we are his. His absence makes no sense.

Okay, listen—let's leave these abstractions to theologians and philosophers who don't pray, because we know very well that sometimes the Lord simply does not provide what we ask for in prayer. The real question is *why?*

What we should never assume is that God acts in our lives only when we ask him. That's ridiculous and wrong. The truth is, God has something to do even with the substance of our prayers. When we understand that, we've come closer to seeing light in the darkness of our doubt.

God plants the seeds for our prayers just as surely as a farmer plants seeds in spring. Our prayers, thus, develop just as seeds ripen. As we grow in our knowledge of God and his promises, our prayers actually mature. Our foolish prayers become purified, the nearer we come to the Lord.

And he gives us time. Growing closer to the Lord is a process in our lives that takes months and years, even decades. Sometimes we learn best when he leaves us to ourselves. His perceived absences make his glorious presence more stupendous.

His ways with us are really a holy training for discipleship. Those who graduate have a diploma from God's own holy school of prayer and faith.

HEARKEN UNTO ME, MY PEOPLE. HEAR MY PRAYER, O LORD!

*Hearken to me, my people; and give ear unto me, O my nation.
. . . Hear my prayer, O LORD, give ear to my supplication.*
—*Isaiah 51:4; Psalm 143:1*

Once upon a time people believed that sound came only from the throat, that our ability to speak to each other was limited by the distance between us—a shouting distance—and that if we wanted to communicate with someone across town we had to hire the postal service or some faithful servant to deliver a note.

That was yesteryear. Today we understand that what the throat produces isn't really noise as much as vibrations, vibrations that miraculously are picked up and "read" by a most delicate instrument each of us is born with—the human ear. We've also come to realize the silly limitations of a "shouting distance."

The telegraph, and later the telephone, extended the distance between talkers immensely by sending those same little vibrations over a metal thread. Metal thread? Who uses a metal thread anymore? Eventually scientists discovered that nothing more or less than the air we breathe was capable of carrying those same vibrations, and soon enough we became capable of "broadcast" communications, a single voice flung out to thousands, even millions, at once.

While such innovations in technology change our lives, oddly enough they also help us understand our God in ways that our imaginations couldn't as easily register before.

Radio communication, for example, helps us visualize how it is that the Lord, whose throne we say is in heaven, can pick up even a whispered prayer in the silence of our bedrooms. The radio is thus even more of a gift of God—not only does it expand our world, it also helps us to understand more about God's power.

What seems clear is that the rapid pace of change in science and technology portends many more momentous inventions. Few of us can even imagine the dramatic ways in which our communications will improve in the next decades. God gives us such advances, in part, to help us understand him better, to bring us closer to him.

But the passages we're considering—"Hearken unto me, my people," and "Hear my prayer, O Lord!"—imply a breakdown in communication. The first line is a call to listen, implying that the people were distracted. The second is a prayer that seems to indicate the believer's sense that God was not giving heed, that he was neglecting the burden of the petitioner.

Isn't it delightful that an instrument like the telephone supplies us with an imaginative way to understand how breakdowns in communication, the breakdowns we all feel occasionally between ourselves and God, can be effectively restored? What needs to happen is quite simple: we need to call. Somebody's got to get on the phone and talk. We need to reach out and touch the Lord.

But real fellowship with God is much more than a telephone call. There may be such a thing as a sweet hour of prayer, but if we communicate with the Lord for only fifteen minutes a day, we'll never have abiding fellowship. To be near unto God requires constant and continuous communication with our source of strength and salvation.

One could argue that life was easier without all the gizmos. It may be that our communication with God suffers in the frenetic pace of the new age in which we live.

On the other hand, wonderful inventions like the telephone can and do bring us closer to God. It's amazing, but an incredible invention like the telephone brings us closer not only to our friends far away, but also to the God of our salvation.

THAT WHICH I SEE
NOT TEACH THOU ME

That which I see not teach thou me.
—Job 34:32

Consider, for a moment, a child—say, twelve years old. She takes praise for her exploits on the soccer field and files it away joyfully in her heart. Her brother makes the honor roll, says nothing about it himself, but blushes lusciously when the fact is brought up around the dinner table.

Although they love praise, most kids don't take admonitions as easily or quickly. Finding excuses comes as easily as drawing breath.

What's notable in kids is true of their parents as well. We all have a bottomless appetite for strokes. On the other hand, only when our conscience is touched by God do we let loose of our pride and admit our failures.

Self-knowledge comes to us in two ways: from ourselves and from God. What most human beings quite naturally desire is what refreshes our self-esteem; what we'd rather not experience is that which condemns our failures. Some of us, of course, don't hear God's admonishment; others hear that voice but don't listen. That's sad.

We can gain all kinds of knowledge by ourselves. By simple observation we can recognize the differences between the almost bush-like branches of an oak, and the brittle, sinewy beauty of a willow. We enrich ourselves, learning more and more about God and his world by examining his creation. Not just individuals but groups of people—communities, congregations of believers, even nations—can grow by understanding more and more about life around them. The kind of knowledge they obtain is willed knowledge, knowledge they want to learn.

But another kind of knowledge comes only by God's hands. Communities and nations profit immensely from gifts of genius and discovery among them. Great discoveries open up new worlds and generate enthusiasm for life itself. Such gifts don't come by chance, but as gifts from God.

The pursuit of issues of depth and truth we'll call *idealism*. Nations who are blessed with idealism grow and prosper. On the other hand, nations that pursue materialistic ends—money, sensuality, self-fulfillment—care less about issues of truth and substance than a schnauzer cares about Rembrandt. Such nations deteriorate and bring others with them down a road to ruin, because pursuing base instincts is the mark of a diseased nation and a diseased soul.

Experience itself is a great teacher, even bad experience. Tragic events can be a blessing when we learn as a people to pick ourselves up after a great fall. All of our experience—good and bad—comes to us from the One who fashioned us in his own image. It is the Lord who in every moment of our lives lifts us up to real knowledge, real idealism.

Our heroes should be those who know God in their souls and yet have an eagerness to learn more about the world he's created, people of great faith and exalted idealism. They know better than others how much of what they have has been given to them by the Father. These people say, with Job, "That which I see not teach thou me."

God, My Maker, Who Giveth Songs in the Night

But none saith, Where is God my maker,
who giveth songs in the night.
—Job 35:10

Some of us envy those who can say they "slept like a rock," because sleeplessness, generally, is no fun. When people say that in sleep they were "dead to the world," often enough they're more than happy that their consciousness checked itself out completely. "I was gone for the night," some say, smiling.

We spend one-third of our lives in sleep; a thirty-year-old is really, in terms of consciousness, ten years younger, most all of that decade spent in a haze. Human beings require sleep, of course, so the necessary recharging of our batteries is hardly a waste of our time or our Lord's.

But the requirement of sleep is something of a mystery. God doesn't get tired, after all, and neither do his angels, according to the Scriptures. The book of Revelation claims that in eternity there will be no night. So the requirement of sleep is something unique to us and quite unexplainable. Why should our strength have to diminish and thereby require us to take up pillows? Who knows that answer?

In sleep we dream, and our dreams are not without meaning. Sometimes they prompt wonderful, creative thoughts. Occasionally, they warm our hearts by reuniting us with people we've not seen for years, some from beyond the grave. At times, they give us accurate portrayals of just who we are. But most of the time, for most of us, dreams dissipate like fog in the morning sunshine leaving, at most, a vague residue, as if we know we've been gone but have no idea where.

For the most part, our sleeping life has little significance for our conscious minds, unless our sleep is disturbed. Sickness, difficult trials and circumstances, even old age alter our daily schedules and keep us from our normal seven hours. The Bible speaks in several places about sleeplessness, and when it does, it always suggests the condition is rich with possibilities. The psalmist says, for instance, "in the night . . . I commune with mine own heart" (77:6). Maybe sleeplessness requires a little study.

To start with, we know that sleeplessness is not simply a nighttime phenomenon. Anyone who can't sleep knows too well that the following day will not be easy. We'll carry tired eyes like excess heavy baggage in the long hours of the afternoon.

Sleep deprivation can be destructive, but maybe it can be constructive as well. If we use our sleeplessness to come near unto God, then our not sleeping glorifies the inner life of the soul and even invites its rest, its own antidote. On the other hand, if we use sleeplessness to wander farther from God, we only enhance our restlessness.

So, how can sleep deprivation be a blessing? Consider the nature of the night. No one's around. Not much is moving. Our work doesn't call us. The stillness, reminiscent of the Sabbath of God, may well be itself a stimulus to fellowship with our Lord. What's more, praying and reading the Word, kneeling before him—these are the first steps toward a morning of joy and comfort. The practice itself anticipates the rhythm of life and death, the night of the grave. Coming close to him as we depart keeps us warm to his touch when we awaken.

But there's more. Night finds us rather, well, unguarded. We're unclothed, in the dark, in need—in the very pose, in fact, that God most desires us to face him—not in our strength but in our weakness.

Our nighttime smallness makes us more fit to meet God because it's almost a rule that in our weakness we come to know his strength. The joy of knowing God cleans the house of the mind of all its cares and worries. God's gladness stills our carping. By his presence in our sleeplessness, he gives us songs of praise in the night.

I CRY, BUT THOU HEAREST NOT

O my God, I cry in the daytime, but thou hearest not.
—Psalm 22:2

Half the world away, an earthquake devastates a city of two million people. Newscasts run videos of ten-story buildings perfectly flattened, entire communities laid waste, freeways twisted into concrete ribbons. Random fires roam like voracious criminals in the devastation. Everywhere there is looting. People without homes, without shelter, their faces full of the numbing effects of shock, sit and huddle beneath whatever shelter they can find. What we see before us is disaster.

Thirty seconds after the news flashes across the screen, you think of neighbors who have a daughter and a son-in-law in that very city. They're close friends, so you run next door immediately to see how they're doing.

All night, you stay up with your friends as, hour after hour, they sit at the telephone, waiting for some word. Time after time they try to get through, to no avail. The State Department tells them that the moment they get any word, they will call. But your friends keep trying. Every time they hang up the phone, the pain on their faces is more noticeable.

When we get no answers—when we ask, when we beg, when we plead, but no one seems to be there—hope fades effortlessly into despair.

Even believers sometimes feel so helpless, so far from God, when no one is there to answer.

Psalm 83:1 complains, "Keep not thou silence, O God: hold not thy peace and be not still, O God!" David begs God to come closer in Psalm

13:1: "How long wilt thou forget me, O LORD? for ever? how long wilt thou hide thy face from me?"

Such difficult times can energize the prayers of those who are what one might call nominally religious. But when they receive no answer, disillusionment can result precisely because they haven't practiced a close walk with God. They don't understand his ways.

But those who know deeply God's presence in their lives have come to know that close fellowship is not something dependent upon their own meager efforts. Such believers know that intimate communion relies also upon God's will. Our own striving is not enough to insure deep and satisfying nearness; God must come to us as well.

Why God chooses at some times to be absent from our misery is a mystery. How, for instance, do we explain what Christ meant when he said, "My God, my God, why hast thou forsaken me?" (Matt. 27:46). All we can do is hazard some guesses at why God is away.

Perhaps we hold some secret sin, a dark inclination of the heart, or even a troubled mind and soul that keeps the Lord away from our distress. If that is the case, then, often enough his very absence pushes us toward a personal examination that serves to cleanse us of our unrighteousness.

Frequent headaches or backaches or pain of all kinds can depress us, hinder our own spirits from the openness so essential to true fellowship, and deaden our ears to his voice. Because this is true, our physical and emotional health is very important.

Perhaps we value our own piety too much. We begin to take his presence for granted, assuming he owes us a walk with him for the sake of our own goodness. Sometimes we mess up horribly, thinking our holiness is the reason for his nearness.

But grace is not a habit or an empty ritual. It is a holy thing, not subject to our whims. God is God, not man. Whatever his reasons for keeping himself afar off, our own experience teaches us that we may well come to value his communion more highly because of those very times when we know, so deeply, that he isn't there.

His absence makes our souls grow fonder. To receive him again, after his withdrawal, bathes our soul in the fullness of his love. Not having him at our side makes his divinity more indisputable. We value his presence more abundantly, having come to know, only too well, the grief of his absence.

SEEK YE MY FACE

*When thou saidst, Seek ye my face; my heart
said unto thee, Thy face, LORD, will I seek.*
—Psalm 27:8

Those who know God use different ways to explain their relationship with him. It seems as if we formerly used phrases like this: "I
learned to know the Lord." Today, the language is different. Today, believers tend to say, "It was in this way that I found the Lord" or "At that
moment I surrendered my soul to Jesus."

Although each of these phrases imply something slightly different
about the relationship between God and humanity, none of them should
be considered inferior to another. We'd be wrong to claim that the old way
somehow lacks something the new descriptions offer.

Which is not to say that we shouldn't analyze our language. "I learned
to know the Lord" does, after all, have some limitations. While it's true
that we don't know God without some knowledge of his being, his
attributes, and his works, and while it's also true that our worship is less
than whole if we don't know God as Father, Son, and Holy Ghost, really
knowing God necessitates more than simply head knowledge.

After all, to have read every last word ever written about God does not
mean we *know* him. Theology and doctrine have real merit, but they are,
at best, a means to an end, only a way of describing the perceptions of the
soul in living spiritual experience.

Wherever doctrine or the principles of theology have a stronger grasp
on our sensibilities than true spiritual experience, those who speak most
authoritatively *about* God are often considered closest to him. Ironically,

but understandably, a desire for mystical experience always flourishes when we start to believe that the way to God is through the mind. Where head knowledge dominates, the soul often goes hungry.

Should we fear the desire for mystical experience? Surely. We can never pin God down by a series of interwoven theological precepts. To know God inwardly is to know him not as an abstraction, but face to face.

What is needed is both theological soundness and mystical oneness. How do we know when we have those in balance? If we do, our service to others will thrive in our communities—and for good reason. Created as we are in God's image, our relationship to other people should mirror God's love to us. Service to humankind indicates that head knowledge and spiritual connectedness are in righteous sync.

Our body speaks a language of its own, but no single part of our physical selves communicates as clearly as our faces. Maliciousness, guilt, boredom, joy, ecstasy—all those emotions appear in detail on human faces. Perhaps that's why the phrase "speaking face-to-face" has the connotations it does. When we look each other in the eye, we expect nothing but the truth. A telephone simply cannot deliver that intimacy.

What does God mean when he begs his people to "seek his face"?

Clearly, he doesn't mean we should attempt to arrive at a physical description. He doesn't want us to make pictures of an old wizened man or any other image. It's flat wrong to think of God's face in an earthly way, because his face is wrapped in mystical dimness. A visible face exhibits what is corporal. God isn't. He is a spirit.

So there is no physical way to see God's face. We can't recognize him, or spot him in a phalanx of commuters. We come near to God in a wholly different way. Our spirit enters directly into the spirituality of God as his Holy Spirit enters into us. What we gain is not a physical description, but an abiding knowledge of the being and nature of God.

At certain moments in all of our lives we passionately seek face-to-face fellowship. Not until we've met God's eye can we rest. Only in that intimacy does the virtual mystery of grace become distinctly and passionately real.

Only then do we see his face.

MY SOLITARY ONE

Deliver my soul from the sword,
my solitary one from the power of the dog.
—Psalm 22:20

(translation from the Dutch version)

Some people avoid crowds at all costs, while others flee solitude like the plague. Some people desire, even ache, to get on every committee they can; others prefer root canals. Some thrive on busyness, scribbled calendars, and an endless array of social functions; others love nothing better than kicking off their shoes and staying home.

Differences in character are marked and noticeable. People who like solitude become exhausted simply by watching socialites trek nimbly through a party of revelers, shaking hands, telling stories, spreading laughter like a happy virus. Socialites look at introspective people and can't imagine where they find their fun.

It's silly for anyone to judge another on social behavior or lack of it. Much of the world's business wouldn't get done if we'd never leave the coziness of our personal space. On the other hand, significant and creative ideas generally emerge from isolation and the depth of thought one simply can't accomplish in crowds.

Despite our differences, each of us has a solitary self, a soul—that which David calls twice in the psalms, "my solitary one." Our souls, our solitary selves, are our precious commodities. Think about it—anything else we own can be replaced. Even our bodies can be destroyed, lowered into the grave. All that remains is the soul.

But even in its individuality and its solitariness, the soul is social. The world can approach the soul, and the soul can approach the world. Our senses, for instance, offer us the pleasure of a sunset so perfect it seems almost heavenly. We hear or see or read the right story, and our tear ducts flow. The soul may be solitary, but it's not without relationships.

However, as stunning as a sunset might be, we don't become one with a landscape. And while we can, blessedly, feel the depths of others' joys and griefs, something in us remains uniquely individual. In marriage, two may well become one; but even in the most intimate of human relationships, nothing is ubiquitous about the soul. It is private, solitary.

The privacy of the soul often creates two kinds of problems. Sometimes we withdraw too deeply in sadness, grief, or hurt to a hideout where even suicide lurks at the gates of our possibilities. We get "the blues" and worse. Despair can threaten a too solitary self. The path toward unseemly solitariness leads to excessive inwardness, self-reflection, even narcissism.

But then again, sometimes we run so gingerly through life that the very essence of the soul withers in the frantic zaniness of our public madness. The soul requires some solitude in order to grow. The path away from self-reflection robs us of deeper thoughts and reflections.

Perhaps we should think of it this way: the soul is much like a tabernacle. In each, there is a general court, where close friendships and intimacy enter. But beyond the gates lies the holy of holies, and no one really enters there.

Except the Lord. He is the only remedy for imperiled souls.

Only God can save us from our loneliness and also give us the society so necessary to the health of our most secluded lives. Those who know God there, in their own inner sanctums, know him most fully and wonderfully. They are nearest to God.

GOD CREATED US IN HIS OWN IMAGE

*And God said, Let us make man
in our image and after our likeness.*
—Genesis 1:26

Our practice of faith, every speck of righteousness we have, every vestige of the religion we carry into our lives—all of it stems from one indisputable fact of our existence: we are made in the image of God.

We can pray fervently, avoid murder, treachery, and idol worship, and do good all the days of our lives. But nothing we do or achieve will make us any more devout or godly. Only when our very souls come into fellowship with God can we joyfully and even effortlessly abide under the covert of his wings.

Think of it this way: every outward manifestation of our practice of religion changes throughout our lives: what we sing, how we sing, what we wear to church, how we pray, even the breadth and width of our smiles. What doesn't change is what goes on inside us the moment we rise in the morning to a consciousness of God's reality. What doesn't alter is our fellowship with him. And that fellowship occurs in a relationship even more intimate than that which we have with any human being. It happens when our souls dwell in God's tabernacle—and when his Spirit dwells in ours.

Even our sin does not alter the fact that we carry God's own image mightily. There's no question that sin has defaced something of what he gave us when he imparted part of himself into us. But our regeneration, something essential to belief, revives that image, an imprint only humans share with the Creator.

In spring, a crocus spears its way out of hardened winter earth and shouts beauty with a sudden burst of color. But we know that beauty only from a distance—like a snowy peak, pure mountain water, a gold crescent moon. We aren't "one" with the crocus. We have no deep personal relationship with the lilting smell of lilac in a soft spring breeze.

When God said, "Let us make man in our own image," what he did was to fashion beings fully capable of close fellowship with him. If true religion is defined most precisely by an intimate fellowship with God, then when God created us in his image, he was creating religion.

Birds are wonderfully blessed with beaks, elephants with trunks, trees with bark, and cats with nocturnal vision—in all these ways God filled nature with glory; but on nothing else in his world did he invest his image. Only human beings can fully *know* his love by intimate fellowship with him.

So what does that mean, really? That we have opportunity to know God like no other member of his created world means at least this: that our warmest and most intimate walks with him are not accomplished for our benefit, but for his. We don't practice religion—don't pray and sing and study Scripture—for *our* benefit. Our righteousness is not our own. He made us in his image, not so that we could enjoy him—although we can; we carry his likeness so he can enjoy us. God gives us his love because we are his, not because of what we are on our own. He wills our lives of praise. He wants to *know* us, in the deepest and richest sense of that word, because we are like him.

Everything we do out of faith, everything we know of God, begins in the fact that we are his kin.

NONE OF ME

But my people would not harken to my voice;
and . . . would [have] none of me.
—Psalm 81:11

The wars waged by Old Testament prophets and New Testament apostles differ radically from those we wage today. Modern paganism wears a different face from the old Baal-worshipers. Today, there are no idols, no physical manifestations of deity.

In a metaphoric sense, we all have idols, of course. A parent can *idolize* a child, for instance. But today's paganism has no pagodas, no high priests, no sacrifices, no high festivals. To be sure, one can find dozens and dozens of covens of silliness—people who think they find meaning in crystals or harmonic convergences. But people in pointed hats worshiping weird deities are not at the cutting edge of contemporary paganism. They are not its soul or its power. Bizarre religious practices are not the real enemy.

The real power in modern paganism is that which is rooted in two beliefs: first, a denial of a personal God; and second, a belief in vague ideals about life and humankind.

In the Scriptures, vying images went into combat. Priest stood against priest on Mt. Carmel to determine the real identity of God. The fires proved that God was *not* Baal, *not* Jupiter, *not* Diana. God was only Jehovah. And his Son, Jesus, is the image of the invisible God.

Today people wince at the thought of a personal God. Not so in the Old Testament, when images of stone and brass implied a personal attention to faith and belief. But today no images rise above the contemporary landscape—no idols, no temples.

But why look at those who deny God? Even some Christians have been affected by the new paganism. Many today are reluctant to talk about a personal relationship with Jesus Christ and substitute vague beliefs in love and mercy, in peace and a higher good.

These beliefs are immortal expressions of the very character of God. But too often in our pursuit of them, we neglect the reality behind them. Love is not love; God is. Like the pagans, we have formed our own view of love and forgotten the source.

God sent his Son as an image. In Christ, the word became flesh and dwelt among us. The *idea* of love is powerless without its source, without Christ. The enthusiasm of the apostolic church—and its successes—was rooted in the reality of Christ, not the ideal. Greeks and Romans pursued the ideals of love passionately, but the apostles carried the living Christ into battle. He was the source of their power and persuasiveness.

In the recent past, an overemphasis on the humanity of Christ eventually gave way to a belief not in his person but his ideals—and once that shift was accomplished, it was easy to relegate the Word made flesh to the back forty. Really, the complaint of the Lord in Asaph's song is his cry today: "My people . . . would [have] none of me." All around us, people respect nature, take joy from art and culture, esteem love and generosity. But absent from their lives is true God-consciousness. He isn't real to them personally.

The battles we face today are both personal and cultural. God's complaints against our superficiality, our vagueness, and the unreality of our piety is, first and foremost, a complaint against our hearts. That's where the battle begins. We have too high an opinion of ourselves, too strong a sense of self-sufficiency. We lack trust. Those are heart problems.

But we have a war outside of our hearts as well, for our culture has denied the personality of God. What we need more than anything is to call ourselves and our world back to an intimate and personal relationship with Jesus Christ.

Love is God, after all. God, really, is love.

A Sun

For the LORD God is a sun and a shield.
—Psalm 84:11

You may have heard loving parents say of their kids, "Our children are the sunshine of our lives." That may indeed be true, probably especially for those who have tried for a long time to have children.

But the happiness brought into life by a child pales in comparison with the far greater joy ushered into our lives by God Almighty. When the psalmist says, "The sun of my life is my God," his testimony of God's love is total and eternal.

The sun is an apt and glorious metaphor for God. When we are near to him, his very presence casts a sheen over all of life and makes visible reality what otherwise would seem formless in the gloom.

From a human point of view, the only really understandable idolatry is the idolatry of the sun. No image, no spirit, no pagan temple can illumine with such fervency, can warm us so fully and bring us such vision, as the sun. It's no wonder that people throughout the ages have looked up in the sky and thought they saw God.

But the words of the psalmist cut through that idolatry: "God is *my sun*," he is saying, not *the* sun.

We might consider ourselves clever for seeing the sun as a metaphor, but God himself has graced this heavenly body with associations that help us understand him. All the theological abstractions in the world don't have the effect of our confessing that he is our sun.

Let's play a bit with the metaphor. The penetration of the sun reaches into the darkest corners of the earth. We don't have to be directly in it to know it warms our world's most shadowy depths.

What's more, even though the sun is millions of miles away, it is—as is evident from our sunburn—very obviously right beside us. Run for the shadows, close up the blinds, darken the room, and still the sun's light finds passage. Even beneath the density of the earth itself—loam and clay and mountain rock—the sun reaches into the depths and warms seeds into life and blossom.

God maintains a home in this gargantuan universe; yet he is constantly in our souls. Our righteousness always blossoms from his warmth.

Imagine a place without the sun. Everything dies, period. Colors fade into darkness. Snow and ice mantle the world. The absence of the sun creates dreariness. And more. Without the sun, darkness flattens our shadows into obscurity.

But when the dawn rises, we measure distances, perceive forms and tints. The presence of the sun enlivens us and our lives, paints meadows like pallets, brings buds to flower, and makes a goldfinch at wing a bobbing stream of gold.

Without God we stagger in the darkness and stumble through life as if careening off tombstones. But his holy magic wand lays light all around us and breaks through the darkness with heavenly clarity.

Our nearness to God waxes and wanes, just as the sun rises and falls. Thick clouds often obscure heat and light. Some days radiate with joy; some seem abysmally long. We have good years; we have bad.

And sometimes the sun burns. Sometimes our own heart's hardness willfully rejects the touch of his hand. If we try to align our souls with God at those moments when our spirits are afflicted by sins we'd rather not admit, then his warmth will ignite into a conflagration. Then there is range fire.

But God, our sun, never reneges on his blessings of light and warmth, even when we harden our hearts. What we must never forget is the promise of glorious quickening he gives to those who know him deeply as the sun of their lives.

UNDER THE SHADOW
OF THE ALMIGHTY

*How often would I have gathered thy children
together as a hen gathereth her chickens under her wings.
—Matthew 23:37*

Isn't it amazing that we can decipher something of the Maker's character in every creation of his hand? A barnyard hen protecting her brood reveals God's characteristic tenderness. But if we sense only God's tender touch on those he loves in the image of a hen scurrying around locating her wandering chicks, we miss the richer associations of the analogy. There's more—there always is.

Think of it this way: where the chicks find protection, under the hen's wings, is, in fact, a God-appointed place. It is right, it is fitting, it is proper, after all, that the chicks be under the hen's wings. Similarly we *should* be under God's care. What's more, it's interesting that as a metaphor for this particular divine characteristic, the Bible uses a winged animal and not, say, a dolphin or a basset hound. Here, as often elsewhere, the Bible uses a winged animal to carry us by analogy into the space between the earth and the heavens.

Such associations are so rich that some mystics foolishly consider worshiping the hen itself. But we can also misuse the God-knowledge Christ gives us in this passage (and elsewhere) in other ways. We're flat wrong if we begin to believe that a hen is only a hen, and that the sense of the Creator's own character is derived only from our minds. The great danger is that we begin to believe that God himself exists only in our minds and *not* in our world. To be near unto God presumes that he isn't simply a product of our imagination or a being who resides only in our hearts. God exists; he is not a figment of a righteous imagination.

Of course, the first step toward becoming as close to God as chicks are to their mother is to deny oneself and admit that only in the mother-God can we really find joy and protection. Self-reliance has to go.

Some find confessing their need relatively easy to accomplish, but then begin, sinfully, to invest themselves not so much in God as in other human beings. "I couldn't live without her [or him]" is language common to our lives. While we need other human beings and profit immensely from their fellowship, leaning too much on others is plain-and-simple sin. God, after all, is our only refuge.

People who know that, who live in that comfort and exhibit the peace that comes with that understanding, are not blessed with that knowledge as a result of their own sharp thinking. They don't know God because they've thought him through. One doesn't come near to God by simply thinking one's way there. It is far more of a mystery.

Also, people blessed with a deep assurance of God's protection do not arrive at their conviction on the basis of the belief that the Lord will always protect them from evil and misery. Evil and misery characterizes much of our lives, with or without God. The peace of the believer is a gift of their assurance that whatever circumstance they encounter—the greatest of joys, the most horrifying grief—God's wings will overshadow them. He will be there.

Now to believe, as some do, that, willy-nilly, they will simply be able to achieve such a vital, living, gracious relationship in times of crisis is plain silly. The believer who knows the protection of God's wings in his or her happy days will know it just as fully in moments of crisis and conflict. Coming near unto God is a behavior that must be practiced.

Those who are at home under the wings of God the mother hen know assuredly that they will pass the night under the gracious and abiding shadow of the Almighty.

THE WINGS OF THE WIND

[He] maketh the clouds his chariot [and]
walketh upon the wings of the wind.
—Psalm 104:3

No tornadoes ever ravaged the plains of Eden; no hurricanes battered its borders. The only winds were likely those which, in the desert climate at morning and evening, carried along a refreshing coolness. Like everything else in a perfect world, Eden's daily breezes came softly and peaceably.

Even the gentle winds of Eden carry something of the Creator's character. The association of God with the wind occurs throughout Scripture. The psalmist claims God walks "on the wings of the wind." On Pentecost, the winds rushed his promised Holy Spirit upon those blessed with his purpose.

In the Middle East, the wind's character is something different from what those in northern climates experience. Its gentle coolness may well have pointed lovingly towards the caress of God's grace.

Of course, no one then understood the peculiar combination of high and low atmospheric pressures that produce the swarming air we come to feel as wind. Throughout Western civilization, fierce winds, coming so unpredictably, were frequently associated with God's reproving hand in our lives. The wind seemed an enigmatic, intangible force. Accordingly, no matter how gentle or enraged its character, the agency of the wind seemed to flow directly from God's open hand.

This idea of God existing in the wind—outside of us—seems entirely contradictory to the idea of God existing in his temple—in us.

We know very well that God dwells in us, his temples. He has chosen our hearts for his home, where he speaks to us—cheers and reproves—in a still, small voice. Our God is intimate and tender, close to us. "Immanuel—God with us" promises that Christ is always with us, his people; and that the Holy Spirit will live in us individually in an even more personal way.

But, if we are to believe Scripture, God the King of Creation also rides the wings of the wind, and the wind bestirs itself very much outside of ourselves. It approaches unobserved, and it comes not simply as a response to our prayers. Like the wind, God comes on his own to awaken us, when and where he wills.

If God dwells in our innermost temple, how can he be at the same time outside us? The only answer to that question is that he is both in and out.

Think of the opening words of the Lord's Prayer. "Our Father" is a description of endearment and intimacy as close as flesh and as lifelong as any relationship we experience. But then comes, "who art in heaven." Heaven is a place apart, not at all within, a place we aspire to, but not the here and now of our lives today. God lives and reigns both within and without.

Insurance companies still speak of natural tragedies created by storms as "acts of God." The swath cut by a tornado awakens astonishment in every witness. God as the wind remains something outside of us, and yet he promises to make our hearts his home.

Some believers too easily give themselves away to mysticism, glorying in the comfort God allows us to know by his Spirit within. When they fix on heavenly things, they lose a sense of God's omnipotence in his world, his kingship, his ruling hand in Creation. God becomes personal, but nothing more.

On the other hand, viewing God in creation but not knowing him personally in the heart risks a frigidity of nature that dies in the lack of warmth outside his personal touch.

Lives given totally to contemplation of the Spirit within make people unfit for their calling in the world, but souls that refuse him entrance to the temples he wants so badly to inhabit never really know him at all.

Here is the great story. Our God is a God afar off *and* a God near at hand. Only those who know him *within* and *without* live in dynamic fellowship with the Creator.

THOU SETTEST A
PRINT UPON THE
HEELS OF MY FEET

Hear my prayer, O LORD, and . . . hold not thy peace at my
tears. Turn away from me that my soul may refresh itself.
—Psalm 39: 12-13

(De Vries's translation)

Stumbling on Psalm 39 can be an absolute shock. Here, David says his soul will be refreshed only if God turns his face from him—and this is the same David God loved.

No greater contrast exists than the disparity between ourselves and God. All religion seeks to bring us together with the Almighty. Yet, in this passage, David, the Lord's anointed, politely asks God to leave and thereby bring comfort back into his life.

At one point during his tribulations, Job feels just as horrible in the presence of God. "Thou puttest my feet also in the stocks, and . . . thou settest a print upon the heels of my feet" (13:27). Job thinks of God as a harassing slaveholder, bringing torment.

Sheer agony is not uncommon, of course, and often enough such torment creates radical change in the human soul. Deathbed confessions occur with regularity. Foxhole testimonies are legion. A date with the hangman often prompts unthinkable piety in even the most obdurate of criminals. Misery, anguish, and distress winnow character.

But David's agony in this passage, like Job's, is of a radically different stamp. Instead of running to God for deliverance, both see him as the creator, in a sense, of their distress. That kind of sheer terror is a species of fear known only to believers.

Job was a saint. Yet, the devil had his way with him. The tribulations suddenly heaped on the man were so agonizing that the only way he could understand them was to assume God had left the premises. What he feels as the horrors continue to increase is that the Almighty, in his anger, is now coming closer and closer and closer, and what he feels is sheer terror. *Because* he knows God, his soul quakes. Only a believer can accurately conceptualize the unalloyed horror of God's righteous anger.

To be near unto God can be understood, after all, in two ways. On one hand, he brings us bliss, satisfies the soul's longing with his love. On the other, however, stands his anger. Only believers understand the dread of his displeasure.

If, in fact, we were all to be dealt with according to our sin, then our collective lot would be to face the terror of his anger. Most of our pleasures and excesses here below don't really rattle the soul, but in eternity our disobedience will be unclothed before the face of God in a place where his awful presence displays itself "where their worm dieth not, and the fire is not quenched." That is hell.

But here below, those who know God's dazzling love have found communion with him, have received grace. Instead of sin standing between themselves and the Almighty, Christ the mediator is there, accomplishing our atonement.

When faith fails the believer, when we feel Christ withdraw, we find ourselves face to face with the naked majesty of God in his anger. At that point we feel the agony of soul so remarkable in the words of David and Job. Only believers can know that agony.

But it is at moments like these that the Holy Spirit enters our lives to erect once again the shield that is Christ Jesus. At that moment, God, who is capable of making his anger flash more violently than the nuclear mushroom, reveals himself intimately to his otherwise desperate children as Abba, Father.

MY SHIELD

For the LORD God is a sun and shield.
—Psalm 84:11

Today, the best we can say for shields is that they make great museum pieces. Nowhere in the world are they used anymore as the armaments of war. Their traditional tasks—catching arrows, breaking the blows of clubs, parrying the heavy thrusts of double-edged swords—are only memories.

While technology may have increased the efficiency of our killing, its advances have, in a way, safeguarded us from the graphic horror of war. Imagine the bloodiness of hand-to-hand combat in which shields are an absolute requirement. Watch, as warriors hack away at each other, one on one, the field behind littered with limbs.

The shield is actually an invention of our instinct. When one is about to be struck, instinct raises an arm in protection, an arm to which the shield is but an appendage.

When we think of the Lord God as our shield, we are mistaken if we assume that God's protection is outside of ourselves and not already a function of the armaments we carry in his world. We wield God, in a way. He is our shield, our defense. He is so close at hand that when our faith lays hold of him, he becomes our own defense.

Hens, as we've said, shelter their offspring beneath their wings. But that idea isn't the intent of this metaphor at all. This imagery comes from what biblical people knew: a shield is something wielded by the individual warrior. It is an appendage, like an arm; and if the warrior wields it efficiently, he will march back from combat alive.

The shield may be little more than a museum piece today, but the imagery is still current because battles that must be fought continue to rage in our lives.

God is our shield against ovarian cancer, rampaging tornadoes, and the shocking horrors of accidental death on the highway. But once again, the shield is not something simply and abstractly wielded by God. We're not benign recipients of cartoon shields that stand and operate on their own. To defend ourselves properly, we must do everything in our power ourselves to gird ourselves for battle.

To "avoid" sin is perhaps too weak a phrase. The shield is in our power. When we are wielding a sword, we do more than avoid sin—we fight it.

In fact, confessing that God is our shield implies our engagement in the fight. It's only by using the shield that we sense the joy and comfort it lends to our lives.

The kinds of shields one finds in museums are often decorated by a name or a coat of arms. The believer knows, however, that only one name can be inscribed on the shield we carry—and that name is Jesus Christ. To carry his shield is to publicly profess our faith to the world.

Saying that God is our shield means nothing at all if that shield hangs in a display of fourteenth-century warfare. We understand the meaning of the line only when we use the Lord's power as a weapon against forces today that seek to destroy us and the glory of our God.

IMMANUEL

But now mine eye seeth thee.
—Job 42:5

Because our understanding of the world around us begins with our senses—what we hear, what we see, what we touch—it's difficult for us to understand exactly what Jesus means when he says, "God is a Spirit: and they that worship him must worship him in spirit and in truth" (John 4:24).

What is real and what is physical is absolutely essential to our living. In order for us to communicate our ideas, we must find associations with the physical world, or else no one will know what we're talking about. Even angels, if they desire to visit us, must make themselves visible and audible, or we'll not know they're there. Some kind of sensory reality is necessary to our life. And nowhere is that better illustrated than in Immanuel. When God literally touches our soul, he does it via Immanuel, God with us.

We're at a park or a restaurant in some other country, when, purely by chance, we bump into someone who hails from somewhere near our hometown. Immediately, a bond is established, if by no other means than language. Even if we've never met before, we're instantly friends because we're alike.

A shaggy cocker spaniel has trotted through the Smith house for years. That dog is as close to kin as anything nonhuman can be. When it dies, something real and definite is lost in the home. Even pets create bonds.

Our old friends and acquaintances, out of our lives for years, show up on our doorsteps, and in a minute it seems that no time has passed at all. Our mutual experience keeps us close. We know them.

Masons, teachers, secretaries, funeral directors—all of them like to talk shop. There's a bond. People who have lost spouses, parents with rebellious kids, Baptists and Mormons and Adventists all share something that keeps them close to each other.

The miracle of the incarnation is that bond God created with us when he pulled on human flesh, when his Son became a user of human language and wore our clothes. In Christ, God laughed. He cried. He was hungry. We don't have to be spirits to know God, because he took on flesh for us so that we could see him. He created a bond with us.

The immense gap between Creator and creature was, in the incarnation, wholly atomized. His human nature was no mask or shroud over a more resplendent spiritual character. Christ's human nature is the means by which he brings Divine life naturally and intimately to our humanity. We know him because of the special gift of creation given to all of us—the gift of his image, an image we ruined by our sin.

But—and here is the miracle—Immanuel, God with us, replaces that of which our own sin dispossessed us. Immanuel brings warmth and life and quickens us from abstractions about the nature of God, because Christ is God—and he is us. With Christ we *dare* draw near to the very Godhead we rejected in Adam, because in Christ we *can*.

For that gift, we owe him our holiness—not only our spiritual awakenings but the very ordinary and homely holiness of our day-to-day lives. We owe him our all.

Immanuel is God's personal touch, the skin-draped point of fellowship with the Father. Through Immanuel, we know God and see him, even as Job did, when he said, "Now my eye seeth."

In the Light of Thy Countenance

They shall walk, O LORD, in the light of thy countenance.
—Psalm 89:15

Around the tree on Christmas eve, the faces of children shine even more radiantly than the colored lights scattered like gems on the branches before them. Even when weddings are celebrated outdoors in the full brilliance of a cloudless afternoon, the lovers' faces can outshine the sun. A man walks off a train, returning from the horrors of war, but his face glows radiantly in anticipation of his family's greeting him there in the crowd of loved ones.

Somehow, the very materials of our flesh display our spirits. Joy beams from the face; sadness reveals itself in darkness.

In God, of course, there is no darkness. Whenever and wherever he appears in the Old Testament, he is always a figure of light—a column of light at the Red Sea, a cloud of light at Jerusalem's temple. Moses is marked as an ambassador of the Lord by a blinding splendor shining forth from his face. For centuries sacred art has expressed this sense of God's light by adorning biblical figures with halos.

Even today the eternal solace that God Almighty gives may be noted first in the radiant glow on the faces of those who truly find him. What they discover in the Lord is never dark; and their hearts, like flower buds, unfold in the soft, undulating light of his grace.

We all know gloomy people who plod through the exercises of faith—praying, reading Scripture, even studying his Word—without a trace of radiance in their smiles. Often enough, there are no smiles at all. They have not discovered his light in their hearts.

People who may once have found God's glory and then lose track of its source go through significant changes that are written visibly in the light of their faces. Their friends all know, on sight, that they're "down."

But we have an unmistakable attraction to those who have truly seen God's face, because the human face that radiates God's glory is irresistible.

Even more irresistible is the very light of God's countenance. The reason is simple: one cannot look at the miracle of grace without flinging away all anxiety. We know God when we see the light of his face. At that moment, his Spirit steals forth and opens our eyes, not to doctrinal presuppositions or creeds, but to the pure and blessed sweetness of his light.

All-encompassing, the light of God's countenance lifts us to a higher level of consciousness, a level at which, miraculously, every last Golgotha we face radiates his glory. The light of God's countenance unmasks every one of our failures and sins. We would be frightened to the soul by being so suddenly revealed if it weren't for the fact that equally evident at that moment is the staggering power of his forgiveness. Only those who have seen the light of God's countenance truly understand the gift of grace.

And what happens to those who find such joy? They *walk* in the light.

"Walking in the light" implies that the radiance of God's countenance is not simply a stage spotlight, something we can move in and out of. "Walking in the light" suggests a world in which God's very countenance shines everywhere we go.

"Walking in the light" means marching away from our own darker visions, as well as those only partially lit. It means hiking out joyfully into the full radiance of his glory.

SEEK THY SERVANT

I have gone astray like a lost sheep; seek thy servant;
for I do not forget thy commandments.
—Psalm 119:176

Wandering searchlights thrown over a darkened neighborhood by a circling helicopter bring a chill to the bone. Yet the lights themselves are an apt metaphor for the eye of God. Wherever he looks, the light of his face makes hiding foolhardy.

But the psalmist is not talking like a criminal here. The image he uses is that of a shepherd's eye rather than a helicopter spotlight. We have here the heart's prayer of someone who is not interested in hiding, but instead wants deeply to be found. The words of the psalmist are the bleating of a heart that knows God but has lost its way.

These are not the words of the unconverted. Only believers understand the nothingness that exists outside the presence of the Almighty. Only believers who have fallen away are capable of the intensity of the psalmist's pleading in this passage.

And it happens. Often. Like this.

We've known God's love. We've entered into the narrow gate and found our path bathed in heavenly light. The powers of the kingdom course through us like something eternally tidal. Forgiveness, we know, is ours. We've walked with God.

But all of that, unbelievably, becomes old hat or maybe too difficult. A seed of doubt grows within the mind—not doubt of God actually, but doubt that what he's given us is enough to satisfy our hunger for joy and happiness. Uncertainty makes the heart restless and comfortless, and the influence of all kinds of things below come to cloud the possibilities God brings to us from above. Our world turns upside down. God is gone. Darkness reigns in the soul. Loneliness possesses the heart.

But then, something reawakens in us. We are gripped by an incredible longing to return to God. From the very core of our souls we search for what, in our flirtation with doubt, we've left behind. So we set a course to return to God's favor and the wonderful touch we have not felt for far too long.

But return is not so easy. When we've gotten ourselves lost, we don't, on our own, find our way back. Our best efforts end in frustration, in near despair.

And that's when we learn exactly what the Lord requires: *We can't do it ourselves.* That awful lesson is harrowing to the self-reliance of the human spirit, but it is an absolute prerequisite to a return to God's love. We come to understand our powerlessness, because all we grasp is this aching void. Our souls come to realize that the agent of our healing is none other than the Lord God we have left behind.

That's when our serious bleating begins: "Seek thy servant."

Just exactly how God engineers our return is itself a mystery, but he accomplishes it through the very ordinariness of our lives. Maybe we read an idea on a page. Maybe pain and suffering bring us back, or hard and perilous times flatten our wills. Perhaps God brings someone of sincere and deep inspiration into our lives. Perhaps he uses something definable only as a vision.

All avenues lead to the same end: nearness. He seeks us and finds us, and once we discover that, our hearts stop their desperate bleating and begin to sing.

Doubt is a sin, but so is the inclination to doubt, the tendency to want more than we have in Christ. Learning that lesson is difficult, even scary. It's very possible for us to draw back in fear from the immediacy of his healing touch. But the posture he wants is a brokenness best illustrated with us on our knees.

The truth is that God hears our cries. He seeks and finds. He will rescue us from a course of life we entertained foolishly. That is the miracle of his forgiveness.

His gracious pursuit of our wandering merits nothing less than our lifelong thanks.

STRENGTHENED
WITH MIGHT

. . . to be strengthened with might
by his Spirit in the inner man.
—Ephesians 3:16

Because breathing is an almost unconscious activity, what we inhale, moment after moment, becomes part of us almost without our knowing.

Air that is dingy or laced with noxious chemicals severely weakens our systems. It enters our bodies through our breathing and even seeps in through the pores of our skin.

Medical doctors advise anemic people to get out into fresh, clean air. Tons of people, every summer, escape the heat by migrating to beaches, where the air seems cool and fresh. Clearly, what we live in affects us.

Golfers know they shoot a better game in the company of good players. A great actor makes a whole cast accomplish memorable performances. Great days invigorate us; bad days are depressing. Our emotional and moral balance is tipped by our experiences from day to day. People who love life's gutters have trouble getting their chins on the curb. If we inhale moral degradation from our culture, we stunt our growth and inhibit the possibility of our becoming all we can be in the kingdom.

But the specific atmosphere of our lives most crucial to growth is our personal relationships, because even *personally* we live in a specific climate. Constant association with those who are morally challenged, let's say, is rough. Sometimes a single conversation with a wise and righteous sage can be uplifting for the soul. We pick up behavior as effortlessly as an accent, because imitation lies at the heart of human behavior.

All religion is, at the core, *personal*. Moses forged the character of the Israelite nation in the same way the apostles' personalities shaped the early church. Luther, Calvin, and others left their personal imprint on Protestantism. In every community, one can likely point at a personality or two who have left indelible marks on those with whom they lived.

The most determining personal relationship of all is, of course, the one between God and a human being. Paul asks that the Ephesians might be "strengthened with might by his Spirit in the inner man." He knows God's nearness is the source of our ultimate health.

We sometimes think that if we could, like the apostles, spend three wonderful years with Christ, our lives would be transformed. But the truth is, he is not gone; he is still with us, daily, hourly, minute by minute. When David said, "I will dwell in the house of the LORD forever" (Ps. 23:6), he meant much more than simply the time he spent in prayer. Most of us spend, what—a half hour a day, at best, praying to God?

But David meant his "dwelling" to be more than that. What he meant was every waking minute. What he wanted in the "house of the Lord" was a reality omnipresent in his life—in warfare and peace, with others and alone. That kind of all-encompassing relationship offers blessedness, inspiration, and courage. It brings life.

Churches who know that are alive. Others, no matter how doctrinally sound, are petrified wood. Preachers who bring this fellowship to worship are ambassadors of God; they don't make noise like cheap cymbals.

God's atmosphere, the holy ozone he brings to us, is so clear and healthy that it swells our chests with vitality. But here's the rub: tell an anemic person to head for clean air, and in an hour he'll have his bag packed. Tell others to find health in God's nearness, and they'll only look at you strangely.

Those who understand the health benefits of a crystal-clear life with God, of a relationship bathed in his pure presence, know very well how great a grace has been given to them.

Bend your knees, as Paul did, to ask that it not ever be taken from you, but that instead you be forever "strengthened in the inner man."

To Whom Is the Arm of the Lord Revealed?

To whom is the arm of the LORD revealed?
—Isaiah 53:1

To know that God is a spirit and that those who worship him do so in spirit and in truth is to be liberated from the dusty realities of this world. All that pulls us to earth and draws us into our day-to-day lives vanishes with our knowledge that God is not here in stone or brick-and-mortar. Riddled by pain or disease, we still can know that God the Spirit reigns. Fearing death is silly; the loss of bodies means nothing. God is a spirit.

As heart-changing as that knowledge is, the confession can be an occasion for sin if we understand it all wrong.

For example, consider the reality of the spiritual world. Today, enlightened minds prefer to believe that demons are silly, childish fabrications, remnants of an ancient myth for primitive people. Obviously, those who believe in Christ know better. When Jesus advised us to pray, "Deliver us from the Evil One," he wasn't talking about an empty concept or a cartoon figure.

Believers also understand that when Christ told us to pray, "Thy will be done on earth as it is in heaven," he was referring to two, actual different places. One is our home for a time, the other the abode of angels. Satan was an angel, and when he fell, he did so in a spiritual world. Therefore, some like to assert that sin itself is only spiritual.

That's crazy. Adultery occurs in the physical world, as does, say, drunkenness. But so do other sins that have less physical manifestations. Some people like to believe that abstaining from certain obvious sins—physical sins—means they are sinless. Nothing could be farther from the truth.

While God certainly is a spirit, he is right there beside us every moment in our physical lives. No one should think of him only as ethereal, an impulse, or a vague and incomprehensible feeling. No, no, no. God Almighty spends his nights at our homes and allows us to enter his tabernacle.

He wants us to think of him physically. How often doesn't the Bible speak of God's face, his mouth, his ear, his footsteps, and the hand with which he gives us his blessing? We know him by these descriptions, and they aren't simply personifications. "He that planted the ear, shall he not hear?" says the psalmist. "He that formed the eye, shall he not see?" (Ps. 94:9).

When the Bible refers to the "arm of the Lord" (Isa. 53:1), it doesn't imply some vague outpouring of power. The actions of God's arm are just as real as if we protected the helpless or warded off assailants ourselves.

Perhaps we should ask Isaiah's question more personally: "Has the arm of the Lord been revealed to you?" The answer isn't in some vague, strange feeling. Have you actually experienced his hand in blessing or reproof?

Jacob actually wrestled with God. Moses actually saw the Creator. But too often we don't see the Holy One ourselves or know him as personally as a child knows her father. We can sing and pray all night long, but God isn't really with us unless he lives in the rooms and the streets of our lives.

God Almighty is a lamp unto our feet as we do our daily rounds. Paradoxically, by way of that lamp, we can actually see, wonderfully and clearly, that which is forever invisible.

THAT THEY MIGHT
KNOW THEE

*And this is life eternal, that they might
know thee, the only true God.
—John 17:3*

Scripture doesn't offer us the record of Christ's prayer life. We can only imagine how active he must have been in prayer—as a boy in his father's house in Nazareth, as an adolescent facing off against the wizened elders in the temple, and as a man, a sufferer and a redeemer, on the road to Golgotha. There must have been thousands of prayers. Just imagine what a great book that would make: *The Prayers of Jesus Christ.*

We don't have that book. Very few of Christ's own prayers are recorded in Scripture, and that fact alone makes what we have particularly precious. Consider this short prayer, for instance: "And this is life eternal, that they might know thee, the only true God" (John 17:3). In these few words lies the entire picture of our happiness, overheard in an intimate conversation between the Father/God and the Son he sent to dwell among us.

It's one of the very few prayers Christ's disciples actually wrote down for our benefit, and it's less an outright request for something than it is an act of receiving. Christ is repeating back to the Father the very cornerstone of our happiness. This is the whole package: that God's people might know him as the one true God. That's what life is all about. That's eternity.

What is at stake here is *purpose.* And Christ is not asking the Father for something new as much as repeating truth he already knows in a kind of thanks to God.

What does it mean? In this short prayer we learn the entire reason for human existence, the blessing of eternity: to know God.

Listen. There is no question that this world offers great blessings. To participate in life itself is a joy. Music thrills us. Our work offers rewards. What greater comfort can we feel than to be loved by family and friends? But at death we leave all of that behind. What is most obviously eternal about our lives is the individual soul, this germ of divinity within each of us.

And that soul, just like our bodies, must be fed—not by vitamins, minerals, and the four basic food groups. The soul requires sustenance after its own eternal nature. If the soul is to grow and blossom throughout our lives, it requires a different kind of nurturing. It requires *knowing God*.

What also is suggested in Jesus' prayer is this: that we enter into eternity not at the moment of death, but already in this life. When our soul is nourished, its poisons are expelled, its needs are taken care of. All of those processes occur as we come to *know God* personally. Therefore, eternal life is not something we only anticipate in the hereafter. It is something we experience now in our intimate nearness to God, for in his light we see light.

Everything we ever have been given, have now, or will receive comes from the Father. God Almighty appoints, allows, and governs all things. But knowing that is not the same as *knowing God*. When God through his Spirit chooses us for his temple, we come to an eternity of blessedness with him even here in this vale of tears.

It is painful to watch nations who don't understand the basic truth of Jesus' prayer. When serious people—strong thinkers—willfully abandon this source of great comfort and truth, it brings us to tears. But perhaps it's most painful to see those who confess the name of Christ but never really receive this soul food, this nearness, this intimacy with God. It's sad, tragic.

But Jesus did not despair. Even today he prays for us the prayer recorded here: "And this is life eternal, that they might know thee, the only true God."

It is good for us to be near unto God. It is eternity to know him intimately in our daily lives.

SHOW US THE FATHER

Lord, show us the Father.
—John 14:8

Christ's own prayer, "And this is life eternal, that they might know thee, the only true God," is a petition to the Father that requires more thought than we gave it in the last meditation. Here again in Philip's request, "Lord, show us the Father," our Savior's prayer is the very foundation of Philip's desire.

The truth about eternity is at stake here. We are deadly mistaken if we believe that our being religious, our diligently seeking him, will somehow be rewarded only with eternal well-being. If that's the way we read Christ's prayer, we're missing the point.

Eternity is not a diploma garnered after years of training and education. It doesn't require a series of projects, some memory work, an internship, and the acquisition of marketable skills. We don't graduate from our preparation for eternity at the end of our lives. Neither is eternity a form of life insurance.

Eternity begins in our nearness to God. Knowledge of God is *eternal*. When we experience him, we already experience eternity. Those who don't know him in life in that intimate way will not awaken to God-knowledge once they've crossed the threshold. It simply doesn't work that way.

Philip's question stands at the starting gate for all of us: "Show us the Father." His request is so naive as to be childlike. Simply, he wants to know God in that eternal way.

Endless doctrinal squabbling only tangles our knowledge of him. Look at the difference between the epistles and the gospels. Already, God's people are wrangling about what's right and wrong, clear and not clear. Even the disciples, after the Sermon on the Mount, begin to grapple about meanings. Wherever knowing God is seen as formulaic, Philip's simple question is meaningless. He's not looking for abstraction; he's searching for the face of the Creator.

The Scriptures throb with humanity's desire to see God, but looking for him can be disturbingly futile. The world is huge, and our perceptions of it are always limited by time and space. Sometimes, while dangerous storms loom over us, sending us into hiding and threatening our lives, people nearby are out mowing lawns under sunny skies. We see only in part, as Paul says. We see only the form, figure, and appearance.

But God is a spirit. He doesn't have a thumbprint or a profile. We don't recognize him by a distinctive walk or a shoe size. Searching for him outside ourselves is futile and even damaging, because idolatry begins when we think we see him. The truly pious folks in the Old Testament world gave their people idols to satisfy a very human desire such as Philip's. The people wanted to see God, so the priests gave them Baal. "Here he is!" Ironically, nothing could have brought them farther away.

The living God cannot be seen on film, in a drawing, or in a series of abstract doctrines. Even though we can't literally *see* him, we know very well the deep urge that lies behind Philip's request, because we too want to see God.

So how can we bring together these mutually exclusive truths? We want so badly to see him, but, outwardly, we cannot.

Christ himself answers Philip: "He that has seen me has seen the Father" (John 14:9).

Our desire to know him, to see him, can be answered only by the Son of Man—God himself arrayed in human form. Christ is our means to seeing God. His Holy Spirit occupies our soul and gives us vision. We can see our Creator by way of Christ's indwelling. We glimpse eternity when we are near to him.

Christ is not the image of God in a temple of idols. The image of God is there in the Messiah.

HE THAT HATH SEEN ME HATH SEEN THE FATHER

Have I been so long time with you, and yet hast thou not known me, Philip? he that hath seen me hath seen the Father; and how sayest thou then, Show us the Father?
—John 14:9

Imagine someone coming to your house, winning the affection and admiration of your children, and then one day, as if out of nowhere, saying to them in your presence: "If you love your parents more than me, then you're not worthy of me" (see Matt. 10:37).

In no time at all, we'd show such a lunatic the door. Some of us would usher him there by the seat of his pants or the scruff of his neck. Others would simply call the police. All of us would think him insane.

The fact is, some of Christ's words are really chilling. But we listen to him, of course, and we don't throw him out because we believe *in* him.

His words, "he that hath seen me hath seen the Father," are absolutely preposterous. If someone in our presence would say something similar— "I am God"—we'd not only shudder, we'd leave the room. The person who said it would likely require protection from believers.

From the point of view of the Sanhedrin, Christ was every bit the blasphemer they accused him of being. What they never saw, what they couldn't see, was just exactly what he told them was there—God in him. They babbled God-talk incessantly, but when Christ stood right before their eyes, they were blind as granite.

Little has changed. Millions and millions of people believe Christ was an ideal man, an example of true piety, a hero of faith, a martyr to the power of love. But that's all half truth. The greatest leap of faith occurs when we jump from admiration to adoration, when we recognize that Christ wasn't simply a wonderful guy but the very God of us all.

Seeing that—that's the key. When we say to each other, "Now you *see* what I mean," we're usually referring to a spiritual kind of seeing, not simply what the eye admits in form and figure. At creation, we all came equipped with that kind of vision. But the fall dimmed our perceptions, gave us all white canes. We trip over our perceptions.

Seeing God in Christ demands an inner recognition that what we, in fact, have before us is not just the world's best human, but someone of truly unique character. We need *to see* something divine, something far beyond our grasp, something immortal and not merely mortal. We need to move, in him, from the finite to the infinite—and when we do, the vision is so overpowering that inevitably we fall to our knees.

And yet, *seeing* the Father does not eclipse Jesus Christ. Think of what the newly married look like the moment they face their families, their vows recited. Pure radiance spreads over their faces. Christ must have carried a luminosity of infinitely more candle-power every day of his life, because his divine radiance was the means by which Philip and others could distinguish God in him. Even for us today, to see that shine, to know God through Christ, recircuits our whole being.

Each of us is unique, and our way of seeing Christ is slightly different. Our human natures are not exactly the same. But Christ, the Son of Man, is, in essence, not an individual, but someone who is part of all of us. His human nature is *the* human nature, and thus only through him, our representative, can we *see* God. He is not just any of us, but all of us. That's what makes him our mediator.

And yet there's more, because the process moves in two directions simultaneously. At the moment we come to *see* God in Christ Jesus, as he begs us to do, God Almighty, in his Spirit, comes to dwell in us. That is the moment at which we draw near unto God and he draws near to us.

To see the Father in Christ is the greatest event of our lives, because at that moment we recognize God. That achievement is the highest aspiration of humanity itself. Knowing Christ fully is knowing God.

WITH ALL THY SOUL

And thou shalt love the Lord thy God
with all thy heart, and with all thy soul.
—Mark 12:30

Anyone who reads the Bible must admit that at times it seems perplexingly contradictory. What are we to believe when David says, "They are corrupt . . . there is none that doeth good," and yet Asaph tells us, "Nevertheless, I am continually with thee" (Ps.14:1; 73:23)? Which is true?

What about this? "As the hart panteth after the water brooks, so panteth my soul after thee, O God" (Ps. 42:1). There is no "going aside" in that testimony. The line throbs with passion for God. How on earth are we to believe that no one does good?

Here's what we know: no human soul, on its own, desires God. Damaged as we are, maimed by our own sin, self-corrupted, we do not thirst after righteousness on our own.

Although many people don't carry a high regard for God, many take religion seriously and practice it steadfastly. But who has not gone into public worship, experienced all kinds of panting and preaching and praying, and yet come away with the cloying sense that a good deal of what occurred was public posturing and church dramatics? How many of us haven't wondered whether anyone, once the sanctuary empties, really carries the reality of God into the streets of their lives?

Those who truly do come near unto God will confess in a moment that their own aspiration to know him is not a thirst that originated in them. What such people always testify is that a thirst for God is itself a gift of grace. Why do some have it and not others? That is a mystery.

But in what forms does God excite that thirst within us? Does it happen through the intellect? By way of the understanding or will? Is coming to God a matter of feelings? Is it borne out of the imagination? Is it simply something mystical?

The answer is, all of the above. How God calls us to him is different in every human case. Some come by learning, some by feeling. Imaginative souls find him in their own visions. Analytic types come by the arrangement of complex ideas. It's always been that way, and always will be. There is no unanimity among humankind, and that fact alone argues for a great deal of freedom of expression in our worship and searching.

Our problem in taking that truth to heart stems from our continual violation of the first and greatest commandment—to love God with all your heart, all your soul, and all your mind. Let's face it, heinous public sin—adultery, murder, theft—prompts its own regret. We know we've done wrong. Shame tells us as much. But who among us really feels him or herself in violation of the command to love him with everything? Very, very few.

What's more, all too often our individual paths to God work against our understanding of our own limitations. We come to God thoughtfully, and we think everyone should. We come to him in intense feelings, and we believe everyone else must find the same path. We raise our hands in praise, and we don't trust those who don't. Those who come to Christ in social action believe all of us should work tirelessly to bring shelter to the homeless, alms to the poor, empowerment to the marginalized. But only a block away, a different believer, someone who finds God through emotional gratification, wants everyone else to feel the same shimmering gratification in the soul as she does.

We are a neighborhood of individuals whose varied perceptions and gifts—good in design and beneficial in expression—create a complex beauty. But too often we begin to idolize the path of our individual pilgrimage and thereby disregard the avenues others have walked as they have approached the face of God.

When Jesus said, "With all thy soul," he meant God wants every last component part of our being. Even the most pious among us need to remember that no single part of what we are should be restrained from the full blessings of his love and grace.

Loving God on our own is quite abnormal. Given our state, then, it's no wonder we have all kinds of problems obeying the first commandment. It's our nature not to.

I SAW ALSO
THE LORD

I saw also the Lord sitting upon a throne,
high and lifted up, and his train filled the temple.
—Isaiah 6:1

"And this is eternal life, that they may know thee, the only true God" (John 17:3). Christ's prayer to the Father is a tremendous blessing for us, explaining as it does how eternity is not only something afar off, but also something in the here and now, something attainable when we come near unto him.

We've already touched on this, but let's examine the matter of *knowledge* a bit more deeply. How do we come to the *knowledge* of God so important for our eternity of blessing? Specifically, how important in our knowing God is our ability to represent him—to draw out his features in our minds? In other words, how significant to our walk with God is our ability to (in a good sense) create an image of him?

The easy answer to that question is that it's not at all important because the task is downright impossible. God is a Spirit, and any attempt to give him form and figure is silly.

But then what do we do with Isaiah's testimony that he "saw the Lord." Was it a delusion? The ravings of a fool?

What we know from his own account is that his vision itself was so profoundly moving that it affected the rest of his life. Of course, those of us who take the work of the Holy Spirit seriously know we can't simply assume Isaiah's vision to be the product of an overactive or unhealthy imagination. The Bible says it happened, after all. We can only conclude that God has, in fact, revealed himself to humanity at certain times—if only a few times. Isaiah saw him. He says it. We believe it. Some learned minds in our world consider our believing Isaiah another species of silliness, but we know there is a whole lot more to our world than some of our leading scientists want us to believe.

One fascinating aspect here is that whenever part of God's spiritual world appears in any way—even angels—it's in human form. Christ himself is called the Image of the invisible God, and also the express image of his substance. We are images of the Almighty ourselves. Why God would choose the human form is quite understandable. If he fashioned us after his image (and he did), then there almost had to be some preexisting shape, right? God is a spirit, certainly, but that doesn't appear to mean that we cannot somehow and sometimes see him.

What's at the bottom here is the difficult distinction between body and soul. They are separate—our bodies die away, our souls live on after death. And yet they aren't—our souls, after all, can only express themselves in the life of the body.

Dreams are our mind's nighttime excursions. Are they real? Yes, and no. They don't really take place in the physical world, yet we certainly can participate in them and feel their terror and joy. Visions occur when we're awake. Eastern people put more stock in the reality of visions than we do, but we can't deny that visions exist. Are these phenomenon part of the physical world or the spiritual? How do we account for what we see of God in our own revelations?

Certainly, God energizes our imaginations and tunes them to the broadcasts he wants us to see—as he did to Abraham and Isaiah. And certainly our ability to see him in these very complex and visionary ways reaches its perfection in the incarnation, in Christ's taking on a human face and body.

Much of this is speculation and mystery. What do we know—really? This, at least. We own an image of God ourselves. In us, something of him is visible. Perhaps what's most crucial about this difficult matter of seeing God is this truth: it is not what we obtain but what we give. The higher God's children stand in the world, the more fully is his image visible to others.

It is when we come near to God that others see most clearly his reality in us. To evidence God's reality, to reveal his image like a movie projector, to show his reality in our lives is any believer's crowning lifetime achievement.

IF ANY MAN WILL
DO HIS WILL

*If any man will do his will, he shall
know of the doctrine, whether it be of God.
—John 7:17*

No one will deny that we grow in the knowledge of God by conforming to his will. And although we come to know him better through our intellect, our imaginations and feelings also aid us in finding him. All of these means bring us closer to him.

What characterizes our particular age is the belief in will, in the ability we have to pull ourselves up by our bootstraps. That attitude or worldview is very important today—much more so than it was throughout history. In fact, one might say that this sort of individualism has become its own kind of religion.

The basic truth of this philosophy is hard to deny. Wherever you look, you'll see leadership roles occupied by strong-willed people. Life is, in Darwin's manner of speaking, survival of the fittest. We all know who's going to make it through the next major conflict: the strong-willed.

This worship of the will has displaced God so completely that the idea of God as the fundamental Will of the universe is viewed as silly. And whenever we believe we've toppled God from his throne, disaster results. We're in bad shape, because without God the world appears to exhibit very little wisdom and far less love.

Even the church has suffered at the hands of this overemphasis on the will as the rule of life. In a mad rush to do things, our confessions (our own statements of truth about faith), for instance, get lost. What many Christians want today is power, especially in the political process. The source of this shift in society is not so much the prevalence of a specific philosophy as what we might call the very dynamics of the human character. Let me explain.

The Reformation was a good thing, but it created its own problems. Soon after the Reformers had introduced change in the European church, orthodoxy—the strict adherence to a firm doctrinal code—ruled with such authority that it overpowered the mystical reality of faith. When orthodoxy turned into stone, mysticism drifted in from the back pew, especially in the eighteenth century in Germany and France. Christendom moved quite naturally from an overemphasis on doctrine to a deep concern with feelings and emotions.

Whenever we put all our eggs in one basket, we are certain to misplace something—and we did. No single Christian organization so clearly represents today's Christian will as the Salvation Army, a group dedicated to doing the work of the Lord. The church today has itself invested deeply into the idea of will, of doing good, and we have sturdy biblical foundations for believing as we do. "If any man will do his will, he shall know of the doctrine, whether it be of God," says the book of John.

An energetic, socially-active faith grew strong, in part, because it was something no one in Christendom had seen for years. Doing good has become the signature of faith. But the real danger is that in our quest for good works we simply hurdle our personal relationship to God to assert that salvation is simply an outgrowth of will, of *what we do.*

In that process, the center of gravity in our relationship to God becomes us and not God. What we do supplants what we are. We judge others not on their heart but on their deeds. We identify our brothers and sisters by their activism, not by their walk with God.

To achieve something in a world motivated by will and good deeds requires accumulating numbers—a tally of souls reached, members gained, churches planted, food pantries constructed. When we run up the numbers, we congratulate ourselves.

There is, of course, some truth to the necessity of good deeds, just as there is some truth to the necessity of a devotional life and a desire for pure doctrine.

But there's more to be said on this matter, and we will return.

INCREASING IN THE
KNOWLEDGE OF GOD

That ye might walk worthy of the Lord unto all pleasing,
being fruitful in every good work, and increasing
in the knowledge of God.
—Colossians 1:10

Two Christians. Ned studies doctrine and the Scriptures constantly, but spends little time on the streets where he lives. Ted could care less about doctrine, but brightens the halls of the nursing home with such regularity that some think he's an employee. Who comes to know God best? Ted, hands down.

The key to the answer is our belief that *eternity* is not just something we arrive at in the moment of our death. *Eternity* is knowing God already now. We gain that *eternity* of his presence right here and right now as we gain a knowledge of him. And truly knowing him means doing his work and will.

Think of it this way. Dogs that live long in our homes come to understand the rituals of our lives and even begin to function themselves on the basis of what we do—they get up at a certain time and wander to the chow when they know we have time to dish it out. Eventually, even our pets come to know us from within. God's imagebearers aren't basset hounds, but there's something to that pattern. By coordinating our own lives by his designs, we come to know him.

Consider what we imply in the Lord's Prayer: "Forgive us our debts as we forgive our debtors." The deal we're cutting with God is quite something. We're begging him to forgive us *in the same manner* as we forgive our debtors. Think about it: what that request means is that we dare ask nothing of God that we don't extend to our fellow humans. In other words, we know what kind of blessing it is to be forgiven *because* we do it all the time.

The forgiveness we want from God is total and complete, and therefore ours must be too. Certainly such forgiveness is more than simply restraining ourselves from doing bad things to those who have sinned against us. What forgiveness means is loving those who have hurt us, and loving them as much as we do ourselves. It's incomprehensible, really—but absolutely required. That's exactly what we want from God—at least that's what we ask him. And we know it because we do it—right?

People sometimes speak about "Christian service"—missionary work, the ministry, volunteering time in the hospice. That's okay. But genuine, inspired Christianity leaves no stone uncovered in its desire to reach all of life. If we spend our evenings at the homeless shelter and think that our nine-to-five job somehow sits outside the realm of "Christian" activity, we're sadly misguided. There's no exclusive list of professions that constitute "kingdom service." Becoming a missionary to Pogo is no more inherently "Christian" than sewing baseball caps, because knowing God is something we do sitting and standing and lying down. We grow in our knowledge of Christ every hour of the day, no matter how our hands or minds are occupied.

In our God, being and will are not two entities, but one. His will is the crystal clear outreach of who he is. If you recite the entire Bible, that knowledge does not mean you know God's will, because the will is within; God's will can be known only inasmuch as our wills become subject to his. One cannot fly a jet via book knowledge. One learns by doing. We come to understand God's will by doing his work.

This kind of practical Christianity—a ministry of deeds done in Christ's name—is not only useful, but indispensable. But it's only part of the whole knowledge of God. There's more to the Creator than his will, and coming to him requires more than simply our will.

Nonetheless, knowing God by doing his work is a kind of double bonanza. Those who are recipients of our work are surely blessed; but then, so are we in the doing. ◈

BESIDE THE STILL WATERS

He leadeth me beside the still waters.
—Psalm 23:2

If the truth be known, the good and faithful believers of a generation or so ago spent precious little time understanding the nature of human will. Although they argued incessantly about whether or not we were gifted with "free will," their investigations often ended right there, as did their discussions.

No matter, really, because our knowledge of God continued to grow anyway; and it did so, ironically, even by the agency of our will. How? Simple. God himself made us grow in knowledge of him. He's not bound, after all, by our sermons or books. He has his ways. The Bible says, "It is God which worketh in you to will and to do of his good pleasure" (Phil. 2:13).

Perhaps because the will is such a wonderful gift, perhaps because it's so powerful, perhaps because misuse of it creates horrendous difficulties—for all of these reasons it's good for us to think a little about the nature of the human will.

That we mature as believers is obvious. Even as the body of believers, as Christ's own bride, we grow in our knowledge of ourselves, of our God, and of his world. What passed as truth in earlier years must be modified by what we've come to understand more recently about ourselves and our world. The melodies the church sings lose their appeal and vitality if what we learn about life and about ourselves is not brought into harmony with what we've always believed. Preaching loses contact with the world, and its power fades through disuse and irrelevance.

What we've been thinking about is how we come nearer to God. That path is difficult to understand at times, but it's not impossible. For instance, in the matter of will, think of our coming near to him this way: the person who bends over backwards to forgive someone who's hurt him comes to know, in his forgiving, the will of God, who has forever forgiven the forgiver. It's that easy. We know something of God by doing his will.

Now some people lack time or opportunity to think about the complexities we've been considering. Some simply lack the brain power. Others work so hard at their day-to-day lives that they have little time or energy for thinking about these things.

No matter. We know very well that no human soul ever earned salvation by the number of hours he or she tallied with nose parked in a book. He leads us all beside his still waters. If knowledge of God is eternal life—as we've been saying—then there must be some knowledge of him available to all, no matter where they stand or sit or serve: in the factory, the kitchen, or the think tank.

Will is something we all have. It acts in us every day. Without it, we're mere vegetables. Like a river within us, our individual wills are always flowing outward, carrying us into life.

Because everyone has a will, it is within everyone's power to have a closer walk with God—provided, of course, that our wills align themselves with his. That proviso is crucial. And when that happens, cruelty disappears from the office, the shop, the classroom. The governor, the farmhand, and the professor all submit quietly and spend their hearts in love. The action of loving others requires no college degree, nor is it dependent on occupying a certain station in life. Everyone can do it.

All our activity here is an expression of our will, and the more closely we align ourselves to the Father's love, the closer we will come to the *eternity* we have been speaking of, the *eternal life* that begins in our being truly near unto God.

WHO WORKETH IN
YOU TO WILL

*For it is God which worketh in you both to
will and to do of his good pleasure.*
—Philippians 2:13

We're right in believing that our wills push us to act, but we're wrong if we think our wills alone prompt acts that bring us into harmony with God's will. "It is God," says the apostle, "who worketh in you both to will and to do of *his* good pleasure."

If we didn't act on our own, we'd be wooden-headed puppets dangling from divine strings. We aren't. Yet, when we do accomplish his work, we do so *because* he works in us—in our wills—to make us want to.

Okay. Now we've arrived at a complex doctrine that some believe simply befuddling. But if we don't try to understand how things operate in us, we're not taking either ourselves or God Almighty seriously. Today, we can buy medical books to help us understand everything from runny noses to basal metabolism. Thousands of people invest in multi-media CDs that define every malady that exists. But where do we find such comprehensive sources for an understanding of our souls? Maybe we ought to pay more attention.

What is the nature of human will? That's what we're considering. When Dietrich Bonhoeffer stood, willing to die, before his Nazi captors, did his will alone prompt him to make that stand? Of course not. His will was also the Lord's.

Perhaps we should think of it this way. Someone who lacks guidance is like a ship without a sailor at the helm. There is no direction, no purpose, no plan for the voyage. Only when a helmsman has tight control of the rudder can a ship stick fiercely to its course.

But there's more here. While the helmsman does the steering, he's not following his own plan. The captain of the ship is the real origin for the ship's direction. He stands higher on the bridge and has a much better sense of where the entire venture is bound. The helmsman's duty, therefore, is to take hold of that helm and steer, but to do so only at the direction of the captain. Need we say more?

But let's keep this analogy afloat for a moment. The longer the captain and the helmsman work together, the better they come to understand each other. The more we practice to do God's will, something already instilled in us, the closer we come to God.

Once more, here's the bottom line. The more we do God's will, the more that will becomes internalized within us. We're way off the mark if we think the Captain is out there, way beyond the blue. The closer we come to him, the more imbedded his will becomes in us. His direction becomes our direction, in part, because of our God-directed *will*ingness.

What's absolutely amazing is that much of this growth happens in us without our knowledge. He's building us up even when we don't hear his tools operating.

But that's not to say that growing in faith and knowledge of God, that coming near unto him, is inevitable. Think of God as a sculptor, creating his work in us over time. Good sculpture demands reshaping: occasionally the sculptor has to whack away at the marble to get the line right. That kind of crash and splinter and splitting is terrible, but it happens. Violent conflicts reverberate with moral shocks that can be devastating.

But what God is doing with his hands on us is creating a masterpiece that is so *because* it holds his very image. What he's designing is not a figure from some glossy fashion magazine. He's shaping us from his very own character. And when this work is going on in us, we are already glimpsing eternity. By the way, if this constant sculpting is not going on in our churches, they'll dry into dust and blow away.

But the work that must be accomplished in us is ours, not just the preacher's. Neither is it something we do simply when we meditate on these ideas. That work is constant, and it is requires much more than head knowledge.

What we do—what we *will* to do—is very important. But we can hardly overemphasize that our *will*ingness to follow God is itself an act of God's will.

WHAT I WOULD,
THAT DO I NOT

For what I would, that do I not; but what I hate, that I do.
—Romans 7:15

At Athens, well-meaning believers erected a memorial to a god they thought they couldn't name. We misunderstand that story if we think that what Athenians were after was simply some unknown deity afloat in the cosmos. The god they thought to honor was a being they likely assumed they *couldn't* know—at least in the sense they thought they *knew* Minerva or Jupiter. What they understood—in some ways correctly—was that there *had* to be a god they *couldn't* understand.

That attitude isn't far afield from some who today call themselves agnostics. Their problem is *not* that they don't believe in a god—that's not the point, or they'd call themselves atheists. What they believe is they *can't*, not that they *don't*. To them, whatever power there might be that creates and runs the universe is simply too grand, too big, too unwieldy to comprehend. So they say they don't know that god because they can't.

If you think about it, that sounds almost pious, doesn't it?

But Christianity stands on the opposite side of a very deeply drawn line in the sand. Remember what Paul said right there at Athens: "Whom therefore ye ignorantly worship, him declare I unto you" (Acts 17:23).

The fact is, we *can* know God.

But let's be fair. Exaggeration also occurs on our side of that deeply drawn line. Some Christians think they know God as inscrutably as God knows them. If that's what we believe, then our reasoning is ridiculous, our best speech little more than stammering.

There is no question about the necessity of our *fearing* God. He is not, after all, a pet, a soft shoulder, or a kindly old gent down the block. However, when we are near unto him, when we know him, our fear is molded by his love so that our relationship is defined by both fear and love. In his presence, our best posture is always a bended knee because we should approach him with awe and love. Talk of God that lacks awe sounds banal and flat. We need his deep spiritual presence in us, shaping our wills.

But God himself affects our wills in two ways—first, by what we come to know in our hearts, and second, by how we come to act on that knowledge. Here is something that happens to all of us: through his will, we come to understand that something we've been doing—say, having a few too many drinks with the gang—isn't what God wants. Knowing what's right is one thing; acting on it is something else. Once we dance into the ballroom of real life, what our will has taught us needs to become *willed* action. That's another step.

Both coming to know the truth and coming to act on it involve real conflict. Knowing what's right demands putting away what's wrong—our old nature. But acting on our belief may be even tougher, because often we fight the formidable powers of the world at the moment we act with God in our hearts. Let's be honest, failure in the second arena happens to everyone. We know what's right, but we can't do it.

When we fail, we often become disillusioned with ourselves, and that's really injurious. We begin to tell ourselves that our struggles with our consciences are futile, that the still small voice in all of us leads nowhere anyway. We may just as well not listen.

Don't ever let that happen. It's much better to fail outwardly than to give up inwardly, because giving up inwardly means shouting down the voice of God within us, hanging up the phone on what God wants us to hear. That's disaster.

What's fundamental here is what's on the inside. We grow and grow throughout our lives; and as we do, acting on what we know becomes easier as we get stronger. Sure, we go backwards and sometimes fall. But we'll learn God's will only by staying close enough to hear his voice.

Real holy pleasure is acting on what we hear him telling us, and that occurs when we are near unto God.

NOT AS I WILL

O my Father, if it is possible, let this cup pass from me:
nevertheless not as I will, but as thou wilt.
—Matthew 26:39

Although Ann's pregnancy had not been without problems, she carried her first child confidently, so sure she was of God's hand on this new life within her. The delivery was difficult but not harrowing with Daniel beside her. Pain? Yes. But there was also a blessed calm, a gift of grace, once the doctor gave her Emily, pink and healthy with life.

A year later, Emily and Daniel were both killed at an intersection not more than a mile from their new home. It's a place Ann can't pass by anymore, ever. She will deliberately drive five miles out of her way and choose to be late to work rather than see the overpass where a distracted driver forced them to . . . but what does it matter how? Everything she ever loved died at that spot. She can visit the cemetery, but she can't and won't pass by that intersection.

The death of her husband and child sent Ann's faith reeling. She had always believed in a loving God and started every day with devotions. Daniel was a believer too. He held Emily one night and told Ann he loved this child so much it was hard to think that the baby really belonged to someone else. He meant God.

For months after the accident, Ann couldn't pray. She went through the motions, even told her pastor, her parents, and her friends that she was doing as well as could be expected. But she knew whatever syllables she aimed heavenward—and there weren't many—were either vicious or never got there. She had always believed in a God of love, and quite simply, there was no way to square what he had done in taking everything she loved with that image. How could a loving God wreak that much horror on the soul of someone who loved him? That's what she thought.

In life, some of us, by God's own hand, avoid such despair; but many don't. Most believers feel horribly abandoned at some moment in their lives. A life that was beautiful goes up in a conflagration, and the image of a loving God is destroyed along with it.

In the Garden of Gethsemane, when Christ said, "Thy will be done," he was asking to be the instrument of God's grace in an action that, personally, he would have much rather avoided. Sometimes when we say to the Lord, "Thy will be done," we are gaining in our knowledge of God, but often that gain costs us dearly.

Ann's attitude toward life and her understanding of God were nearly destroyed. Before the accident, everything was wonderful. An overwhelming sense of happiness kept her soul aloft in joy and praise, so great was the love of the Father. The Lord had seemingly made her the center of his life, bestowing blessing after blessing. Sadly, this notion of God was false through and through.

Our horrendous burdens utterly destroy such false faith, but build a new one, a stronger one, one more appreciative of the omnipotent power of God Almighty. Ann needs to become aware that God is not at our beck and call for whatever happiness we need, that he doesn't measure the course of things via *our* desires, and that his plans include more than our personally drawn itineraries for our lives.

When Ann learns that the God she has loved and worshiped is much, much bigger than her own sweet perceptions, when she begins to understand that the only way she can come to him is on her knees, when she learns to submit fully to his will, even as Christ did on Gethsemane, then she will learn the immense reality of God. Then she will know him.

And at that point a whole new education begins. At that point, the troubled heart, understanding its weakness, comes humbly before the Almighty. The will to drink the cup, as Jesus did on Golgatha, to drink it with a broken heart, and to thus cooperate in God's work and attune one's will to his, is to find eternal life.

Our entering into God's great will for his creation, whether it be through joy or sorrow, is our honor and the self-exaltation of our soul. He becomes our peace.

I LOVE

I love the LORD, *because he hath heard*
my voice and my supplications.
—Psalm 116:1

L ots of us know very well how being bitten by love can send us reeling. Love seems so overwhelming, so unreasonable in its power, that we melt to everything else.

Sometimes that intensity proves dangerous. Spouses are unfaithful, sweethearts wander, and what was once ecstasy spins horrifically into the worst kind of agony. Frighteningly, people often pull the triggers on their own lives when their deep affections are not returned in kind. Chest-throbbing love is almost mystical in the way it takes us out of everyday reality and becomes an obsession. It abandons reason so fully that it reaches its ends in only two ways: full reciprocity or death.

This kind of love is the stuff of romance novels and feel-good films, but it's not really uncommon. Ordinary people—you and me—can be transported into some otherworldly state by untiring dedication to love.

The *Song of Solomon* sketches such ecstasy in detail; in fact, the Scripture throughout uses this kind of intense love to explain and define the nature of the relationship between God and his creation. Marriage is the best way for us to know the powerful tie that bonds the Creator and his people. Jehovah calls himself Israel's husband, after all, and tells us he has *betrothed* Israel in righteousness. Whoring is infidelity to God. In the New Testament, Christ is the bridegroom of the church.

Want to define love's ecstasy? Look at Christ's own description: "And thou shalt love the Lord thy God with all thy heart, and with all thy soul, and with all thy mind, and with all thy strength" (Mark 12:30). That's total love. We are to be consumed by our attraction to him.

The example works two ways actually. In knowing God's love, we're more able to know how to love each other. The Bible is a kind of how-to manual when it comes to love. Our relationships are exalted and made holy when we understand the character of love given as grace to us. What's more, this pattern helps us understand how, when we break the contract, despair stands at the door. What results is the worst of evil from the best of blessings.

Psalm 16 begins with this song: "I love the Lord." Yet, in the original, the idea is more gripping because the utterance is simply, "I love." We'd say it this way: "I'm in love!" People who trumpet that phrase to others often seem in orbit.

But our love for each other is only a copy. God's love for us is the original. And arriving at the state of knowing deeply that we are loved isn't simple or simply willed. It is what we've been speaking of as coming near to God, and it only comes after some searching on our part. When our homesickness hasn't been cured, hasn't found calm, and when we finally return to God, we fall really in love.

Tons of people don't dislike God; many like him, even if they don't know him. What's not to like, after all?—God is good and kind and offers us blessings. But admiring God and respecting him are not at all the same as *knowing* him. We're talking about a relationship and an intimacy that leaves theoretic knowledge in its dust.

Holy passion is ours in being near unto God. "I love"—in these words the soul is aflame. This love, available now, is yet eternal. And yes, in a way, by the world's standards, it's even somewhat unseemly.

But it's not total yet, for one day the wall of separation will crumble, and God in us—and we in him—shall attain the perfection of the holiest love ever.

THOU HAST NOT REMEMBERED ME, NOR LAID IT TO THY HEART

And of whom hast thou been afraid or feared, that thou hast lied, and hast not remembered me, nor laid it to thy heart? have not I held my peace even of old, and thou fearest me not?
—Isaiah 57:11

Love seems so simple, a blessed state of mind and heart we simply fall into. Loving ourselves, after all, comes quite easily; and loving God doesn't seem too tough either. Our only difficulty is in loving others, and our problems with that stem from the fact that other people are generally ornery. Isn't that right?

When Christ said the first and greatest commandment was to love God with all your heart, with all your soul, with all your mind, and with all your strength, he did so not because loving God was easy, but because it wasn't—and still isn't.

It's sentimental and silly to think that years ago the world was full of righteous people. While it may appear so—after all, today there is certainly more unbelief in the air—one hundred years ago human beings found it just as difficult to follow this commandment as they do today. In fact, the prophet Isaiah describes a very human condition when he says of the people, "Thou hast not remembered me, nor laid it to thy heart."

Let's make this perfectly clear: knowing what *loving God* actually means is of crucial importance to the believer. And the first step is to understand that it is not at all easy.

Love means *giving*, right? People conceive of love as an act—giving alms to the poor, clothes to the naked, power to the dispossessed. Love is demonstrated when we take something of ourselves, something precious, and give it away to others who have need.

But God has no needs. He isn't begging to be the object of our benevolence. What we need to bring to him is more than our gifts; what he requires is every bit of us. We are, after all, fundamentally his already, created in his image.

Keeping anything of ourselves from him is a form of robbery, since somewhere buried in us even deeper than our DNA is his image. We *are* his. We are not our own. To believe that we love God as some being outside ourselves is outrageously wrong. Such an idea actually accuses and condemns us. To love God fully is to walk with him so closely that he isn't "out there."

What's more, our desire for a closer walk originates in him. He plants our needs, then exerts the pressure that turns our wills into his and brings fellowship and honest, open prayer. When that kind of fellowship characterizes our whole lives, then we've begun to obey the first and great commandment.

You'll notice that nothing is given away here. There's no sacrifice, no penance, no charitable, tax-deductible donations. Loving God consumes heart, soul, mind, and strength. By coming near unto him, we are only returning to our source and doing so as shamefacedly as a thief who, on his knees, humbly begs forgiveness.

Love loves symbols. A ring is perhaps the most universal symbol. But most people also have private museums of their own, stocked with this or that token of this or that night together, mementos of love which, by their own physical existence, usher us back to a time and place when love itself bloomed. Ah, yes.

And so it is with the prophet's line: to lay God upon the heart is a symbol, a token, a remembrance of the commitment we made to give ourselves to the Lord. It is held in a secret, holy place where we know it will be kept fully and eternally. Loving God means giving something to him all right—it means giving him everything because we are already his.

There are not three or four easy how-to steps here either. The only means by which God becomes the focus of our lives is by our melting away in him. To love God in the way of the first and great commandment is to be inwardly consumed by the love that he himself pours into our hearts.

We know how hard this commandment is to follow when we consider how many people we know who have made such a deep and intimate commitment. Not many. But that deep commitment is what loving God is all about. And that's why we're here.

WITH ALL

Thou shalt love the Lord thy God with all....
—Mark 12:30

Many believers have little trouble doing good. Every church on the block has some form of outreach, doesn't it? It may be that the second commandment Christ gives—to love our neighbors as ourselves—is easier than the first. Certainly loving others is more popular than doing what the first command demands—loving God with every last particle of our being.

If you want to see raised eyebrows, try telling people busy doing good works for their neighbors that they should love God more than they do. Yet, that is the first and great commandment. Reversal of the two can be fatal.

Why? It's unthinkable that anyone who truly loves God in the way Christ commands would not love his or her neighbor. The first commandment generates the second, after all. But that's not true when reversed. Millions of people do good things, are kind and charitable, yet could care less about God Almighty.

Doctrinal purity and a life of good works are great blessings, but we need to remind ourselves again and again that the very heart of faith is blessed fellowship with the Eternal Being. At the core of fellowship is our all-encompassing love for him.

But reaching that love is tough, because at the heart of the commandment are the two words at the top of this page: "With all." To love God with heart, soul, mind, and strength is a project only a few of the holiest of saints ever truly accomplish.

Why? Sin. It has estranged us from God, set us at such a distance that the job of loving God "with all" is too formidable and its requirements far beyond us. How often can we claim to love God with everything in us? Not often—and certainly not continually. If the heart of the commandment is total commitment, who's really arrived?

But a few distinctions are in order here before we sell ourselves off to despair. The fact is, sometimes God works his will in us even when we don't know we're up to his work. There's that to consider. It happens.

And this. Even the holiest martyr, at the moment of his death, might be estranged from that kind of all-encompassing love by the sheer horrors of his human pain. Nearness might not always be possible.

One more idea. The moment a mystical, all-encompassing love for God steals us from this world, we lose at the second commandment, don't we? Some who desire such union end up zombies, dysfunctional in the world God loves.

But the command itself still stands—"with all." Now answer this: who on earth has ever accomplished the full range of this command without failing once?

Only one. You guessed it: Jesus Christ.

What's more, only Christ obeyed the second commandment just as fully—to love your neighbor. The real crown of Christ's glory is that he did, throughout his life, both love God Almighty and other human beings—and he did this with every bit of his human consciousness, his human heart, his human soul.

There is no success for us without him. He is the shield lifted over us. Because of him, the Father tolerates our ineptitude and our sin. With him, we receive divine love.

None of our parents or grandparents or friends have ever qualified *on their own* for all of the blessings of grace. But even though in life they may have failed to measure up, in Christ they come spotless before God. And so will we, when in death we all fully die unto sin and come near unto God. Then we will know him even as we are known.

What kind of superglue holds us to this promise? What is it in us that keeps our eyes on the goal? Not simply our love for God—that's mottled. Not simply the fact that we've experienced him or that we occasionally do his work—that's tarnished with sin too.

The mystery and blessing of the Christian life is simply this: that the fire of our enthusiasm to stay near unto God is kindled only in Jesus Christ, the Son of God Almighty. He not only keeps our eyes on the road; he delivers us to our destination.

WITH ALL
THY HEART

Thou shalt love the Lord thy God with all thy heart.
—Mark 12:30

The heart, a pear-shaped, muscular, little-more-than-fist-sized organ whose contractions are entirely self-stimulated, pumps blood to all parts of the body from just left of the center of your chest, where it sits in residence. But that's not the *heart* the Lord was referring to when he gave us the first and great commandment.

That heart is much more difficult to define, because it's not an organ as much as it is a function. Examine a cadaver and you'll find pancreas and liver, intestines and bowels. You'll also find the heart—but not the whole *heart* God wants from us.

So what does God mean? We might think of it this way. The heart is the source of our feelings. Its fluttering and pounding excites us and brings us joy, but only those feelings that emanate from the soul are of lasting consequence. The heart, itself a gift of God, functions *with* the soul, which is the center of our spirituality. In fact, the heart is indispensable to the soul.

We should never forget that our love for God begins in him. Our heart drinks in his affection, and his love enters our soul. That process awakens our own ability to give that love back, again through the heart. So the heart is *not* the soul, but it is necessary to the soul's function. Its ability to register religious feeling is the door by which God enters into our innermost being.

So it is, therefore, the medium by which God draws us near unto him. He is, after all, the omniscient, the all-powerful one; and when he extends his love, we are as powerless as steel filings before a massive magnet. We are drawn to him fully and exclusively, the way the sun draws a bud from the ground in the spring.

The heart is the source of our affections—and of course we have many affections. We can be overwhelmed, for instance, by something as static as a mountain landscape. A waterfall can take our breath away. We can love morality or science or just about anything that is noble and of good report. But that kind of love doesn't fully satisfy us; the soul needs more.

Many of us love pets, because pets give affection in return. But there's more. There's love between friends, between siblings, between parents and children, all even more reciprocal forms of love. Marital love is so wonderful and strong that the Scriptures use it as a metaphor for the relationship between God and humanity.

But even marital love does not fully complete us. Our souls find real peace only when the affections of the heart are aimed and connect at an even higher level—at being near unto God.

But how can anyone suggest that love between God and humans is reciprocal? It isn't. God calls all the shots, after all. In fact, he doesn't even need us. If one of the characteristics of love is a shared relationship, then love between God and human beings isn't possible at all.

Without Christ. Jesus Christ came to make the unequal, equal. In Christ's love for us, in his humanity, we can carry back to the Father what it is he demands from us—the love of our hearts. Not just piecemeal either, not just chunks, but fully, as we are loved.

When we come near unto God, it is only through Christ. He makes it all happen.

WITH ALL THY SOUL

Thou shalt love the Lord thy God . . . with all thy soul.
—Mark 12:30

If you have been a believer for a long time, if you know the first and
great commandment like the back of your hand, if the words of this
verse have been part of your understanding since you were a child, then it's
not difficult to feel more than a little guilty for not living up to it. But stay
with the idea here for a couple of minutes. Just listen up.

Look, had people really obeyed the first and great commandment, the
roots of true piety would have dug deeply into the soul and stayed there.
Love is, after all, the greatest good; and love for God is the greatest love.
What's more, when love for God is strong and true and grows from every
square inch of our being, then love for others naturally follows.

But loving God isn't as easy as it sounds. In part, that's why Christ
breaks the action down the way he does, separating heart from soul, soul
from mind, mind from strength. Had he simply instructed us to love him,
we could have idealized the commandment away. Instead, he insists that
we must love God with heart, soul, mind, and strength.

Intense pain begins in the sensations, in the heart, in the feelings. If that
pain doesn't subside, then by its own awful persistence it can eventually
reach the soul, leading to despair. Similarly, it's the heart that admits love's
joyful stirrings; but once admitted, love must settle deeply in the soul in
order to grow. The heart feasts on love and fancies its impulses; but love
wouldn't have much substance if it were to go no deeper than the affections.

Without an ear, we can't hear. But that doesn't mean that the instrument of the ear itself is what listens. We listen with our hearts and with our souls as well. In fact, that which we really hear, that which affects us deeply, gets beyond mere affections.

We can be stirred to the bone by an engaging movie. A half hour after it ends we can still feel the intensity of the world we saw before us. But a day later, those feelings dwindle when life hauls us back into its ordinariness.

Affections change. One sees it daily, hourly. A parent can be moved to tears by the sight of his or her child crying. The kid laughs, and it's over.

Some people get perturbed if the Lord's name is dishonored and appreciate Christ's occasional stirrings in their hearts. But if that's the extent of their pursuit of God, they are more committed to their own good times than they are to being near unto God. They love God—maybe they do. But they don't love him in the character of the first and great commandment.

Here's *the* question: do you come to God because you'd rather avoid something eternally unpleasant, or do you come because you want to be near unto him? The love that Christ commands isn't transient or partial. It isn't prompted by our choosing to avoid the flames of eternal darkness, nor does it come from some hidden corner of who we are. God's own want to be near unto God simply because they want to be near unto him.

And yet, this first and great commandment is so overwhelming and exhausting, so gigantic, that we cringe because we think it's impossible.

And it is. That's why we have a Savior. We will have peace in our souls in spite of our lack of belief if by true faith we are tucked neatly away in the person of our Savior, Jesus Christ. Then we will be near unto God. Then we can love him with everything we are. Christ makes us conquering lovers.

WITH ALL THY MIND

Thou shalt love the Lord thy God with . . . all thy mind.
—Mark 12:30

On Valentine's Day each year, people celebrate love by giving sweets to their sweethearts in boxes shaped like the caricature of a human heart. Most Valentine's Day cards also plant that plump icon somewhere, making the heart as ubiquitous as the pumpkin at Thanksgiving or the witch at Halloween. The heart is love's most famous symbol.

To understand that loving God demands the heart takes no great effort. But what of mind? The mind's functions include thinking, dissecting, categorizing, analyzing—actions not generally associated with the selflessness essential to loving others.

But the mind is more than an instrument of reason; the mind includes our consciousness, our creativity, our imagination, and our ability to reflect and meditate. Consciousness is a uniquely human gift. Not all creatures are blessed by God with this ability to understand (somewhat) themselves.

It goes without saying that not all human beings are equally blessed with consciousness. Each day some children are born with less than adequate mental abilities, and they grow into adults without gaining a much greater sense of themselves or their worlds. But such people can and do love God with all their hearts and all their souls. In fact, many love God with all their minds as well, no matter how limited.

Such people are models for all of us. It makes no difference where one's IQ range begins or ends, the requirement of the first and great commandment is the same: love God with all your mind. No investigation into any area of life should be undertaken, then, without a conscious appreciation of this fact: that at the controls of creation's turbines stands the Creator and Sustainer of the universe. If the study of biology or geopolitics, quantum physics, post-modernism, or ancient Chinese culture begins with God out of the building, then we clearly aren't working with the total commitment Christ demands.

Everyone has some sort of view of the world, some ethical or moral and religious porch from which to look out at all that we can see and know of God's creation. What is of utmost importance is that God Almighty does not stay in the kitchen or the study or the family room when we view the world from that porch. If God doesn't figure into the equations of our worldview, then no calculator will function properly, because we aren't listening to the first and great commandment—to love God with heart, soul, *and* mind.

But our mind's capacity is not limited to our personal concept of God. To *think* Christianly—and to do so deeply—requires a comprehensive understanding of history, of doctrine, of science, of what is known in many, many areas. History itself is a blessing.

And yet, loving God with the mind is more than imbibing academic knowledge. We *do* far more than *read* on any given day. What we eat, how we choose to spend our leisure time, how we behave when working—these things are the work of the mind at a very personal level, and they too need to be considered in our understanding of loving God. Our time is Christ's time, all of the time.

And yet, beware. When we too urgently seek to do God's will, to think Christianly, to want to love him, we'll have trouble. If we try to be Christian to avoid hell's heat, we'll not succeed. Our every moment will be blessed with the love of God *only* when our actions emerge from great thankfulness for his deliverance, for his gospel of good news.

One doesn't put on Christianity. Pushing and yearning will get us nowhere. Coming near unto God is a matter of knowing deeply how much he loves us and then giving him our lives in thanksgiving.

Love for God that comes from the heart and soul is very much a matter of his planting. He is the source of our own devotion to him. But the mind is slightly different. We can train ourselves to think about him deeply, to work at accomplishing his will, to structure our lives in such a way that praise is in our every step. That process itself will bring us ever closer to God.

WITH ALL THY STRENGTH

Thou shalt love the Lord thy God . . . with all thy strength.
—Mark 12:30

L ove is the very essence of the gospels, isn't it? In fact, if you compare all the world's religions, what's common to them and universal in its reality is love itself. It makes me nervous to read through the Old Testament, with its macabre rituals, its barbaric warfare, and its avenging God. And Paul—some of his invectives are simply insulting. They wouldn't be there if the Good Book had had an enlightened editor. Love is the whole truth. It's the one word worth building your life around. And Christ is love's most endearing example. Love is all you need, as the Beatles said.

Sound familiar? It's easy to idealize love, and today we have a penchant for doing exactly that. Love *is* the first and great command—that's not a lie. But love is not simply an ideal. It's a practical reality that Christ makes most definite when he says we must love him with *all our strength*.

He is not talking about gathering one's strength and giving one's all for some feeling, some grand idea, some vision. What Christ asks us to do is give of ourselves in the touchable existence of the real world. He wants our muscles and tendons. Our power is what he's after—the very circumstances of our strength. For what? To love him.

The last thing we should do is buy into some kind of false spirituality. God's not asking us to invest our strength in religious things, in visions and ecstasy, in feelings and warm fuzzies. That's not it at all. There are no special "spiritual" categories into which he wants our strength deposited.

A doctor can love God with all his strength just as fully as a preacher. A carpenter can give God all his might just as gloriously as a missionary.

God's own greatness isn't limited by our professions, nor does it concentrate its efforts only on the saving of souls. God's almighty love permeates every inch of our lives, and it expresses itself most fully when we show that love with our various talents and professions. Every inch of this creation belongs to him.

A sculptor gives thanks in her work, just as a preacher does. A lawyer glorifies God in the courtroom just as substantially as a Christian teacher in a classroom. No callings are omitted. A dairy farmer who holds church office serves God as fully in the milking parlor as in the council room. Motherhood is a calling fully as God-glorifying as mission work. Nothing stands outside his reign and authority. He wants our strength in his world.

But we err in at least three ways. Many, many people hide their talents and don't use them for the kingdom. Some are stubborn, some simply skittish, but all violate the first and great commandment when they set their talents on the shelf.

Wrong use also occurs frequently. Some work their fool heads off and busy themselves with their jobs until late into the night; but when the goal is self, not God, then such uses of human strength are just as much violations of the command as not using our talents at all.

Others abuse what they've been given. Make a list of talented people who use their imaginations, their dexterity, their beauty, their wit for the opposite goal of what the Lord intends—to bring disfavor instead of praise to God. For instance, think of the millions of dollars funneled into movies that slam God's name. Abuse is omnipresent.

What's important to remember is that this great commandment isn't being sent to those who *don't* believe. It comes to us, his people. And what we know, even when we fail in the enterprise of holding fast to this command, is that the Lord will not relent in his expectations until the scales fall away and we begin to understand that our love for him has to emerge from heart, soul, mind, and every last bit of strength he's given us. Obedience is that all-encompassing, that comprehensive. He wants, in short, all of us.

Simply by knowing that fully, we will find rest in him.

HE THAT LOVETH
NOT, KNOWETH
NOT GOD

He that loveth not, knoweth not God; for God is love.
—1 John 4:8

A chill sets into the church when people begin to claim that a sturdy set of doctrines will bring us to a knowledge of God. Knowing God has its source in our very identity; we are, after all, his imagebearers. Our knowledge of him grows as we learn more and more to bring our will in line with his. What's more, our knowledge of him matures in often surprising revelations. As if he were a clown, he startles us with his face in the middle of our deepest and even most dreary distractions.

On the other hand, if we think that knowing God has nothing to do with creeds, we're wrong. Without a foundation, we're bound for silly mysticism and bizarre New-Age-like fantasies.

To grow in our knowledge of God requires our spiritual experiences *and* our doctrines *and* more. We come to know God by loving others. "He that loveth not, knoweth not God," says John, "for God is love" (1 John 4:8).

Consider forgiveness. Really, the most difficult question any of us face is this: can God forgive our sins? Can God forgive not simply those acts that defame us in front of others, but our very condition? How can we be made right before God when we are what we are? Really now, can we be forgiven?

There's an angle in the Lord's Prayer that's helpful here: "Forgive us our debts as we forgive our debtors." A command is embedded in the words

Jesus suggested: we must love as we want to be loved; we must forgive as we want to be forgiven.

What is suggested here is that we learn by doing. We come to understand the mystery and miracle of God's forgiveness by forgiving those who have wronged us. We come to know God in the act of loving others. We learn by our own experience.

But don't overestimate yourself. The forgiveness here described is no trifle, and certainly not the action of some overworked officer for a two-bit crook. To forgive petty wrongs is no more difficult than shooing off flies.

Real forgiveness is more than simply excusing someone, because real forgiveness requires soul surgery. We need to be opened up, painfully, as if with a scalpel, and have that which is diseased cut out. God is that surgeon, and what he cuts away is our sin. Our growing in knowledge through forgiveness is not something we set out to accomplish on our own. God is the source of our ability to forgive others—let that never be forgotten.

Look, the real test of our powers of forgiveness happens when we take aim at those who have really made our life miserable, who have spread lies, stomped on our toes, made our waking and sleeping hours bitter. There's the rub. To forgive someone like that—not because it's our duty but because we (of all things!) love those people—that's the test. It's impossible, you say? Yes, it is—on our own. It simply isn't natural. But that's the job—take it or leave it. After all, on the heels of the first and great commandment is a second like unto it: love your neighbor as yourself. All too often, our neighbors are enemies.

So how do we do it? Only this way—by loving *what is of God* in every human being. There is something of God in everyone, after all. Even the thief on the cross saw Christ's radiance in the depth of his suffering. We can love even our enemies for the germ of God's essential being that is in every one of us, for the eternal destiny planted in his or her soul. That's what there is to love.

No matter how evil people become in life, they never lose something that is divine. That is the point of connection between us, the point where grace may rush in.

That person who learns to love—and to forgive—his fellow human travelers comes to know something of the eternal, something of God Almighty.

CLEARLY SEEN AND UNDERSTOOD BY THE THINGS THAT ARE MADE

For the invisible things of [God] from the creation of the world are clearly seen, being understood by the things that are made, even his eternal power and Godhead.
—*Romans 1:20*

Occasionally believers experience something of the Almighty in events in their lives—the miracle of birth, the freight-train might of a hurricane or tornado, the sensuous beauty of a rain forest, the breathtaking spectacle of a sunset in a broad and open sky. Nature is, after all, a deep and ready source for knowing the God whose handiwork it is.

For centuries, believers have asserted that God is knowable in two ways: first, by way of his Word, the Scriptures; and second, by way of nature, his handiwork. But being cast into awe by a tumultuous mountain stream or the play of the northern lights is not enough, on its own, to bring us near unto God.

And while some like to say that the church itself is made irrelevant by the beauty of fresh snow on an evergreen forest, truly coming near unto God from the sight of the sublime beauty of nature requires a vision, a view of life itself. Let me explain.

In nature, we see something of the Lord's power, a vision of the eternal. We are awestruck by nature's power, by its sheer beauty, by the way, ecologically, it manages itself. What truly amazes us, however, is the understanding that we too have been created with similar manifold riches, with beauty and power, with untold strength. When nature's beauty prompts us to see ourselves as the creation of his hand, we've arrived at the second stage of the realization required to know God in his creation.

At that point, however, we sadly confess our failings. We know the deep smudges of our own sin have dirtied our faces, marring whatever grandeur was there at the beginning. But to languish at the reality of sin is to jettison Christ. Those who truly know their fallenness, know the reality of Christ's sacrifice for us. Our smudges, our dirtied souls, are washed clean in his blood.

Call it a process and not a phenomenon, if you will, but that kind of vision is necessary to come to a knowledge of God through a lakeshore dawn. The pattern we're talking about here follows, after all, the stages of creation. In the beginning, God molded the firmament, dotted the dark skies with stars, lit the sun into flame, and made the whole wide earth wiggle with delightful creatures. Only then did he fashion humankind; and only after we fell from that beauty did he send his Son to die for us.

What must be said, time and time again, is that the Eternal Being is not invisible. We are told that we shall see him and know him, even as we are known. We don't come by that knowledge through doctrine, but neither is it ours by some kind of mumbo-jumbo mysticism. What it takes is a kind of vision that sees nature, ourselves, and the incarnation in every last leaf and snowflake.

The truth is, God *does* reveal something of himself through the world he's created. We sense his power; we delight in his play. But as beautiful as nature is, it's not the finished masterpiece. It throbs with his beauty, but we shall someday see even more.

Standing on a mountaintop is exhilarating, but seeing the beauty of his world as a palace without a God is an eternal letdown. The Creator gives song to the meadowlark, brings foam to strong surf, calls the sun to rise each morning. He lights the skies with stars and planets, and his voice blasts in thunder.

That person whose understanding of nature, of self, and of Christ enables him to feel the life of God in the play of light streaming in a forest sees and knows the divinity of his almightiness and thereby visits the glory of the Invisible—that person comes near unto God.

AND THE SECOND
IS LIKE UNTO IT

And the second is like unto it, namely this,
Thou shalt love thy neighbor.
—Mark 12:31

E ven pagans have asserted that God is visible in nature. When the poets of the Scriptures say that God is in the thunder and lightning, that his rage is manifest in an earthquake, it's not hyperbole. Nature is a stage for God's drama. In it, he allows himself to be glimpsed as the curtain undulates. Seeing him there is a blessing of eternal worth.

It's not difficult to understand that truth because all of us have been thrilled by nature's incredible beauty. What's more difficult, perhaps, is to know that God is also visible in humanity. It's probably tougher to see the sublime on a street corner.

The theory of evolution asserts that humankind has evolved from plants and animals, from every living thing. Even though what is at the base of this theory is a disbelieving mind, something of its pattern is borne out by Scripture. What Darwin himself would argue is that a human being is the pinnacle of nature's achievement, because in humankind, complexity is strikingly evident. While it's true that human beings are the crown of God's creation, we didn't emerge, alligator-like, from a swamp. We were created.

But Darwin's not wrong: we are different from flora and fauna. We have self-perception, a will, a thirst for holiness, the spark of genius, an ability to appreciate the beautiful, and a clear consciousness. We desire the ideal, we sense the eternal, we embody a score of characteristics no other creature has.

Nature helps us see God—there's no question. We know the architect by his work, the poet by her songs. We know God by his handiwork.

But what about humanity? Even though our sin has broken the mirror of our God-likeness into thousands of pieces, something is yet attractive about us, thrilling in our possibilities. The image is darkened now, like an old glass, but it's there.

Let's be honest. It's easier to love a landscape than a curmudgeon. Often, we'd rather not deal with the guy next door. Our relationships with other people can make us bitter, send us to our rooms to hide.

But if we think of what humankind has done, what's been imagined, what's been thought, what joy there is in so many things, then we come to know that, even today, human beings are imagebearers. Consider Abraham Lincoln and what he did in leading a torn nation through war to love. Consider the change Martin Luther King brought about in the minds of an entire nation, how he brought us to see our sin. We can do wonders.

Love! We're capable of it. What's greater? Something in us longs to be one with someone else. That desire becomes so strong we willingly over-look others' faults. Who cares? We want to love and be loved. We experience it and want more.

With the Spirit's prodding, our ability to love spreads into family and friends. Our love for one person does not in the least diminish our capacity to love many others.

But what of love for those who are not family or friends, for those who hate us, who use us, who hurt us? We can love them when we come to see that every human being has something reflective of God. No one ever loses God's image completely. It is that element of the eternal, that bit of God, that piece of Almighty character that demands our love.

An ancient vase, something that belonged to a great-grandmother, is inadvertently broken. Do we throw out the pieces? No. We sweep them up carefully, knowing that even if it is broken, it still holds something dear.

Love for neighbor means holding dear that which is divine in all of us. Knowing that image in each of us is knowing God.

The second commandment is, thus, like unto the first.

THE IMAGE OF THE INVISIBLE GOD

[Christ] is the image of the invisible God,
the firstborn of every creature.
—Colossians 1:15

We shiver with awe at the glimpses God allows us of himself in nature. And because we are created in God's image, we can also see something of him in humanity. Nonetheless, we see and know him best where God defines himself in line and form and action, and that is most explicitly accomplished in his Son, who took on human flesh. The invisible God is most visible in Jesus Christ. Through Christ, we *see* the Creator.

Some feel they can know God in nature—in trees or sunsets or crystals. Others assert they can know him in the character of their fellow human beings. But because the most complete image of God is in his Son, any attempt to know the Creator without Christ will be a species of idolatry. "No man . . . knoweth . . . the Father save the Son," Christ says, "and he to whomsoever the Son will reveal him" (Matt. 11:27).

Let me say it this way: Christ *is* glory. We name ourselves after him—Christians; he brings us salvation. His redemptive work is recorded in Scripture and still goes on. The course of world history is decided by a nation's being for him or against him. Peace lays over the land in his name. Good families turn dysfunctional when they neglect him.

Some claim him to be a great prophet, another Buddha, Confucius, or Mohammed; but when they do, they undermine the Christian religion and even the development of the human race. That's a lie, after all. Any attempt to shade his glory brings night to the soul.

And while it's forever true that in Christ we will receive eternal life, we should remember that the blessed accommodations of heaven are only furniture. The glories of eternity are not pearly gates or streets of gold. *Glory* for real believers is in knowing God face-to-face, in having that intimate fellowship. And that glory is, through Christ, already here. In Christ, we sense something of the glory of eternal life—now, here below! Eternity is not something that comes along only at the end of life. Eternity begins in our knowing God *here*. And we can know him, most fully, through Jesus Christ.

How? Through Scripture. Even though he's long ago ascended, the record doesn't lie. He was among us. Read his story, and he still comes alive. Our imaginations bring him into our living rooms. Listen to him speak, marvel at his parables, and it seems he is here with us, addressing, admonishing, encouraging, and comforting us—just as he did with his disciples. The story makes him real.

But his essence isn't just in the story, the written record. He's given us part of himself, his Spirit, a flame of love and sacred purpose that glows in his people. Christ came two thousand years ago, but he's not gone. He's here in us. He knows our names. We understand him from the Bible, *and* we recognize him in our hearts.

Now hang on, because here's the crowning achievement: Christ, the image of the invisible God, doesn't merely charm us with that image, doesn't just show it to us to make us marvel. That's not it at all. What he's up to is his own sculpting job. By showing us what he is, he's taking what we are and shaping it, molding it, giving it form and substance to this end: that the very image of God we seek, the substance of the Father, is itself made more perfect *in us*. Through the work of the Spirit, he's making God visible in us.

On this earth, we can come to no greater knowledge of God than that which is created when Christ, himself the image of the invisible, renews that very image of the same invisible God in us. Hallelujah!

HALLOWED
BE THY NAME

Hallowed be thy name.
—Matthew 6:9

Most of us get irritated with silly little name tags, but try to imagine an important meeting where no one knows anyone's names, where everyone is simply "Sir" or "Madam" or "You at the end of the table." Doing business would be awful.

Even though today there are millions of Scotts or Theresas or Lees, names still personalize us. If you want to distance yourself from people you know, just forget their names. You want to make God impersonal, call him "the force."

When we call upon "Our Father in Heaven," we're defining a relationship in those very words. We're personalizing God and the nature of the relationship that exists between us. That relationship is not vague or foggy or whimsical. What exists between us is defined by the name we use when we call upon God.

Let's stop here for a moment. For the most part in these meditations, we've been thinking about the inner life, the feelings, the religious sensibility that knows the reality of God in our very core. All along, we've been saying that doctrinal purity doesn't amount to much without the inner conviction that God lives in us. But there is an outer life as well, something we've been calling our "consciousness." Maybe it's simplest if we call these two approaches head knowledge and heart knowledge.

Here's the problem. Christians everywhere spin their wheels trying to get to a knowledge of God by one of those ways. Some claim to know him by the way he excites their hearts; some claim to know him by understanding his attributes and his ways. The church flourishes when we value equally our knowledge of him with our feelings for him. But Satan loves torturing our harmonies, and the history of the church is pockmarked by distortions of one kind or the other.

Make no mistake about it—feeling God within us is a gift of inestimable value. Without it, we never come close to him. But as a feature of God's image within us, the consciousness far excels the feelings, because the consciousness thinks through the emotions our feelings bring us. Flowers feel; so do pets. But only human beings have a consciousness that takes up the cause of the universe, judges and decides about phenomena, and acts on the basis of what it determines. Through the consciousness, we can take up our kingship, for by consciousness we act and rule.

But what do we mean by a "consciousness of God"? Let's begin where we started today—with the name of God. For naming him begins our quest to know him. Picture consciousness this way: a woman is struck by a sense of God within her, struck in fact, to her knees. She bites her lip, opens her eyes heavenward, and seems lost for words. "How do I address him?" she asks herself, and the words that follow seem most meaningful: "Father in heaven. . . ."

As we've already said, that phrase defines our relationship. God is as close as a loving parent, as far as heaven. With his name, we begin to consciously understand and know the Lord our God.

Mysticism—simply feeling God—without consciousness is chaos and darkness. Our naming God—our use of consciousness, in other words—brings light upon our path.

However—and this will come as no surprise—frequent repetition dulls our perception of what we're saying. When the name of God is repeated as if by rote, its meaning becomes empty. Habit dulls spiritual consciousness.

But when there's a crisis, something big happens. For the first time in years, we pray with a whole new knowledge of what "our Father in heaven" really means. The reality of God is impressed upon us, and even as we speak, we think through what we're saying.

Here's the bottom line: if we enter our discourse with the Father with any less consciousness, any less attention to what we're doing than when we turn on our computers to begin our day's activity, we're not hallowing the name of God.

And indifference, as all of us know, simply won't be tolerated.

The Name of the Father, and of the Son, and of the Holy Ghost

... baptizing them in the name of the Father,
and of the Son, and of the Holy Ghost.
—Matthew 28:19

If we were each required, publicly, to list all the names we use to address those with whom we are most intimate, many of us would blush. Lovers have pet names for each other, parents have pet names for their kids, and most people even have goofy names for their pets. Such names are usually seldom repeated outside the walls of our homes. In fact, some might argue that there is a direct relationship between level of intimacy and silliness in names. The reason is simple—we define our relationships by what we call each other.

Consider for a moment the word *God*. What it means is a highly exalted being who transcends human puniness. The word itself doesn't point clearly at any relationship unless we affix *my* to it. Then it has meaning and relationship.

How about *Most High?* In Scripture, the phrase is often used by idolaters. What it indicates is a quality or proportion, that our God stands higher than anything else. But the phrase really doesn't, on its own, bring us into fellowship.

What about *Almighty?* It suggests protection and refuge, and like *Rock*, offers the sense of a shelter in which we can pitch our tent and not worry about wind and hail.

Jehovah is an expression of the Being of God, and like Almighty it suggests a being far greater than ourselves, a power who makes our finiteness an embarrassment. But then our mortality is embarrassing, isn't it? There's nothing lovely about growing old. Everything about us moves slower and slumps lower. Each day brings intimations of our demise. We don't hear as well, and our vision gets fuzzy. And yet, something in all of us wants so badly to live that we'll sometimes settle for any kind of immortality. That's what makes some people crash in mid-life crises. We simply don't want to go into that dark night, gently or angrily.

In all of this mess stands *Jehovah*, the forever, the I AM. He is what endures. On our own slippery slope toward senility, we know the God of the omnipresent—the I AM—is omni-lively. He's our fixed point, the eternity of our old age.

And what about the word *Lord?* Suggests servanthood, doesn't it? We are his property, the sheep of his fold. We take his orders and appointments.

Perhaps the most value-laden address to God is *our Father*. And the reason is no more profound than this—that we are his children.

In addition, however, the fatherhood of God suggests that he is always near and dear, that we are his name-carriers, that despite the joys of life our real home is with him. He is our Father.

But there's more. For if we think of the reality of the Trinity, we learn more about God and his relationship to us. And what we come to know is this: God as *father* is no mere metaphor or comparison aptly penned by a writer of old. No. There's more to this name than a suggestion.

What we know is this. Long before creation, the Son, Jesus Christ, was with the Father. Long before Adam inhaled his first breath or Eve hers, there was family and relationship. Our own concept of parenthood was born out of the very character of God. When he created us in his image, he gave parenthood to us, gave us family because he knew it already. To know God as Father is not to simply guess at his attributes. He *is* a Father. He is *the* Father and was so before time began.

And here is the blessedness of salvation—we *are* his children. We are not simply *like* his children—*we belong to him*. That's the joy that we carry eternally.

Look, if somebody feels that the doctrine of the Trinity is just a convenient philosophical strategy for answering difficult questions, they're wrong. That God *is* Father delights our soul and gives wealth beyond any here on earth. That's the truth.

Who Dwelleth on High and Beholdeth the Things of the Earth

Who is like unto the LORD our God, who dwelleth on high,
who humbleth himself to behold the things
that are in heaven, and in the earth!
—Psalm 113:5-6

Although "familiarity breeds contempt" is not a line one finds anywhere in Scripture, the truth of the matter is that, in some ways, it could be found there. As strange as this may sound in a book titled *Near Unto God*, we need to understand that when we violate the distance between us and God, we bring on God's contempt.

In order to be near we must keep our distance? This sounds confusing. But it isn't, really.

Who can deny that often in life our neighbors are best viewed from afar? "Good fences make good neighbors"—that's what another old axiom asserts. See that beautiful new church on Fleetwood? It bustles every Sunday, works busily all week long. But when we start to attend, we discover that the senior pastor and the youth pastor haven't spoken to each other for months. We'd rather not have known that.

Does that mean we shun familiarity? No. The bond that the Scriptures continually use to describe the relationship between God and his people is marriage, the most familiar of relationships. Who knows our weaknesses and peculiarities better than our spouses? Yet, when marriages work, they create the very best environment for love that we know. Familiarity doesn't *always* breed contempt.

The Lord's Prayer begins with these words: "Our Father who art in heaven." In the very first words we bring to God in this model prayer, we establish a distance. We don't say, "Our Father who dwells here in me," even though that is also true. We show our "creatureliness" by acknowledging our Creator. We bring him our humility by looking above where he reigns.

People talk about their "private space." It's irritating to have others violate that invisible barrier with "in your face" conversation. From the bottom of our hearts we want to be loved, but we can only be comfortable with the familiarity of those we ask into our intimacy. We feel uneasy with those who "try to be" our friends.

That God, Creator and King of our world, actually comes to live in our individual hearts *is* the good news of the gospel. That a Being of such loftiness would slum with us is the miraculous testimony of his love. But he wants to be reverenced, nonetheless. And as politically incorrect as this phrase is in contemporary society, with respect to God Almighty, *we need to know our place.*

And what is our place? We are the receivers of God's grace. He comes to us. He entered the garden after Adam and Eve fell. In Christ, he laid himself down in a manger for us. At Pentecost, he sent his Spirit. We don't grab grace. He gives it. Our place is to receive it. It comes from him, from above—which is not so much a direction as an indication of God's character and being. For he is and always will be *above* us. Understand that and we *know our place.*

In fact, only when we understand that are we capable of bringing him our love. Then we become not only recipients, but actors in the process. "Unto thee O LORD, do I lift up my soul," says the psalmist (25:1). We bring our lives before him, only after we know his grace has come into our lives. Knowing God is knowing he *first* loved us.

Efforts to bring God down to our level—whether they occur in the language we use to him or of him, the songs we sing, or the images and the trinkets we create seemingly to remind us of his grace—bring us only his contempt.

We come near unto him only by grace, by his gift, by his coming to us. There's no room for our pushiness or arrogance or manipulation in that confession. What he wants is our humility.

BEFORE I WAS AFFLICTED, I WENT ASTRAY

Before I was afflicted I went astray:
but now have I keep thy word.
—Psalm 119:67

People like to say, especially in moments of deep distress, that suffering builds character and strengthens faith. And it does. But not all the time. What's more, believing that it does when one is at the moment of crisis isn't particularly easy.

Suddenly and without warning, an entire town falls into ruin at the hands of the crunching and grinding earth shifting. In the earthquake's aftershocks, dazed people stand on the street in the grim ruin of their lives and wonder deeply about a power much greater than themselves. Some come closer to God at that moment than they have ever been before. But once the mess is swept away, the new houses rise, and streets are repaired, the wonder and the questioning departs. Life goes on. Order returns and with it, indifference.

Suffering also prompts atheism. A child is sick with cancer. In shadowed corners, families hold hands and come before God, pleading for life. But the child dies, and it seems all the prayers were for naught. That the soul rebels at unanswered prayer—at the seeming indifference of God—is understandable. Nor is it difficult to see how some might say that if God exists, he cannot be a God of love. How many people were really *lost* by the Holocaust? Maybe millions. Where was a God of love? Who can forget the stinging words of Job's wife? "Curse God and die," she told her husband in an effort to relieve his suffering.

What we must remember is that whenever nearness to God results from a walk through the valley of the shadows, God Almighty makes that nearness happen.

What seems clear is that suffering purifies only an already believing heart. Only that soul who *was* at one time near unto God can admit with the psalmist: "Before I was afflicted I went astray: but now have I kept thy word" (119:67).

Let's make a quantum leap for a moment. What also seems clear is that prosperity and pleasure *never* bring people closer to God. Two cars in the garage, a hefty savings account, a healthy family, a tree-shaded home—these things make us feel entirely self-sufficient and secure. We stand on a lush green lawn and admire the work of our hands. In our opulence, we need to be prodded to remember God.

Think of Solomon, in all his wisdom, gone to pot.

What's true of us is true of families and of nations. Comfort and ease weaken character, drain away our dependence on a power greater than ourselves, and fill us with the idolatry of self-reliance. The rich man or woman who can stay near unto God is someone who likely was close to him before wealth intruded. Inevitably, what he or she comes to recognize is how mechanical our faith can become when we live in luxury.

In whatever shape our life is materially, if we know that Satan is fully capable of toying with us, of leading us into pits and pestilence, yet *also* are confident that God's reign is secure, then we can be content. That doesn't mean all prayers will be answered to our liking. Inconceivable deaths occur and do so with frequency. Much-anticipated miracles don't happen. We suffer. The world can be a bad place. Things fall apart. Good people do awful things.

But if we know the big picture—that God reigns—then we know that even if here below we have to lower a child into a grave, we will someday come to see the glory of God's face. Someday his reality will be revealed, and we will know him intimately. Someday we can say with the psalmist, "Before I was afflicted I went astray: but now have I kept thy word."

To thy name be the glory.

WITH THEE THERE IS FORGIVENESS, THAT THOU MAYEST BE FEARED

But there is forgiveness with thee, that thou mayest be feared.
—Psalm 130:4

Luke tells the story. Jesus is invited out to lunch by Simon the Pharisee, but it's hardly a private session. Seemingly uninvited guests show up, including a woman from the shady side of town who, rather garishly, begins to wash Jesus' feet with both her tears and a special brand of alabaster she carried along in her supply of potions. Simon the Pharisee saunters over, raises an eyebrow, and then reminds himself, snootily, that he didn't ask Christ over to do the kind of public slumming presently going on at his place.

Christ tells his host, "to whom little is forgiven, the same loveth little" (Luke 7:47).

Simon the Pharisee likely didn't take kindly to the mini-sermon. But we should, even though the truth here must be approached delicately. In one corner stands Simon the Pharisee, honorary consul, head of local Lions Club, married to chair of the annual Christian school telethon. In the other, a hooker, her saddlebags full of condoms. Hardly a fair match, right?

But Christ says the hooker really *loves*. Now Simon has to be taken aback by his guest's unpleasant response. After all, he'd invited the itinerant preacher over for lunch. Wasn't that a show of something? Sure. But Simon never got down and dirty and washed Christ's dusty feet. The woman did. The person who knows deeply the truth of forgiveness, knows deeply how to love—that's what Christ tells him.

The pattern is simple: first sin, then forgiveness, and then our love. From this pattern we gain a deeper knowledge of God. That's what we've been talking about here—a knowledge of God. But arriving there is a dangerous business, because sin is the means.

Listen! Our fall from grace in the garden changed absolutely everything and everything absolutely. There's no doubting that. But we'd have never known the immense character of a forgiving God had we not fallen into sin. It's true. We know more about him because he has forgiven us. We know far more than angels do, after all.

Every deeply moved utterance of God's love in the Bible springs from the thrilling experience of forgiveness in the heart. We'd not know reconciliation or sanctification if we hadn't been delivered from misery in sin. We know God because of our sin.

Believers and unbelievers frequently differ right at this point. What often goes along with unbelief is a refusal to believe in the reality of human sin. After all, who needs God if we can do it all ourselves, right?

Fashionable Christianity downplays sin too. People who have been solidly brought up in a Christian fellowship can easily downplay sin; but when they do, they also erase reconciliation. Forgiveness doesn't mean much if there's seemingly no dirt to erase. For fashionable Christians, good works and high ideas become the soul of Christianity. If, as the psalmist says, "Blessed is he . . . whose sin is covered" (Ps. 32:1), then fashionable Christians know nothing of this grace.

But those who have been brought to their knees know and know deeply the cleansing joy of forgiveness, the quality of mercy. They know God's love.

Should we sin, then, that grace should abound (Rom. 6:1)? Of course not. People who say that don't love God at all. It's an insult against divine love.

But what this idea argues for is that each of us have a deep and abiding sense of our own sinfulness. If you hold yourself erect and think yourself a saint, you'll never know forgiveness, you'll never know God's love, and you'll never give it back to his world and his people. But if you understand your sin and seek forgiveness, you'll know in your heart the deep commitment of Christ's own promise of love and joy.

Those who know their need of God know him better than those who don't, because they know what it is to be forgiven.

When it comes right down to it, that's nothing more or less than the gospel.

I Acknowledged
My Sin

I acknowledged my sin unto thee ...
and thou forgavest the iniquity of my sin.
—Psalm 32:5

That we come to a greater knowledge of God through our sin is a truth we stubbornly resist and with good reason. What's more, it's fair to say that Satan relishes messing us up here too, begging us to misunderstand or misapply that knowledge to our lives. It may well be that had Adam and Eve not fallen, God in his mercy would have found another way to reveal his character. But our reluctance to buy into the idea, as well as our speculation about what might have been, doesn't negate the truth: through sin we come near unto God. After all, just because the idea isn't easy to accept doesn't mean it's wrong.

If we separate redeemed believers into two types, some of this may be clearer. Take Peter, who blatantly denied Christ three times after being warned specifically that he would. On the other hand, consider John, who never departed as radically from God's way. Both are believers, but of a different stripe—as are Salome and Mary Magdalene.

This difference creates an odd irony. Those who have *not* fallen away and returned sometimes envy those who have. That jealousy is understandable but mistaken. What we need to remember is that we gain a knowledge of God through his forgiveness *only* by making an assessment of our sinful heart. Sometimes big-time sinners, those who have messed up most publicly and horridly, pinpoint their problem only in that big-time sin. They fail, thereby, to understand that human depravity goes far deeper than a few actions, no matter how horrendous. On the other hand, those believers who've not violated the commandment in the most dramatic and heart-stopping ways know, by their frequent examinations, that the nature of human darkness is much more subtle than a few mistakes.

What is shared by both kinds of believers, however, is the knowledge that God alone teaches us the nature of our sin.

Most of those who don't know God still have something of a conscience. Even if they don't know why a certain act is bad, they start to feel lousy about doing it. For those who don't believe, the conscience still acts as a guide and often brings them to a more moral lifestyle.

But the process isn't exactly the same among the redeemed. With believers, the first knowledge of our sin startles us, as it did David when he was accused of adultery and murder. Immediately, believers wish whatever it was they did could be recalled. They wish they'd never done it. They stand embarrassed and ashamed before God.

All believers pray. And when they do, those who know their sin face a huge decision head-on. They can hide and only perpetuate their lousy guilt; or they can open themselves to grace. They know very well that praying demands honesty. "When I kept silence," David says, "my bones waxed old through my roaring . . ." (Ps. 32:3).

But David went on to confess. In all of us also that breakthrough, that triumph, ushers in blessedness through a sense of God's holiness that's unimaginable.

The Chief of Operations here, however, is God himself, who engineers our pilgrimage to grace. The holiness he gives us in his forgiveness brings light to our path and makes our steps firm.

But here's what's most important. Don't think of that light as a spotlight, stage right or left or parked in the balcony. The light he gives to illumine our paths is generated from within us. *We* are lit up by his holiness. He gives us a tangible knowledge of our sin *and* his grace that we know from the inside-out.

That eternally comforting knowledge of God comes from being near unto him. And that's how it is that even our sin works to our greater knowledge of God Almighty.

WHEN GOD
SHALL JUDGE

For we must all appear before the judgment seat of Christ.
—2 Corinthians 5:10

How many millions and millions of people don't take God at all seriously in their lives? Add to that the number who, while asserting some belief, really don't practice any sense of faith or worship. Then think of the millions more who only go through the religious motions—attend church, pray habitually, do good works. The number of people who really seek a knowledge of God, who want in this life to see his face, who desire like nothing else to draw near unto him, and who practice coming closer and closer to God—that number, we have to admit, is vanishingly small.

It's amazing, isn't it? One can only imagine how painful such unsubstantial figures must be in God's sight. He created all of us, after all, blessed us with life and care and subsistence. Yet how many really seek him—I mean, really? Very, very few.

But all of us, all of the billions who ever lived, will stand before him one day in judgment. On that the Scripture is clear.

How on earth will God pull off something as colossal as Judgment Day? Answers to this question have been silly, to say the least. Some wonder where billions of people could assemble, what kind of continent that would take, what kind of PA system would be required? Some say that a thorough-going review of every last action of a person's life could take years. Simply to review one family could take centuries.

Where silly questions are asked, unbelief is likely the source. Art—poetry and painting—has really messed us up here. It has often drawn a caricature of the judgment.

Actually, that day will require little more than a settling of accounts, a practice any accountant—or anyone who balances a checkbook—can understand. Think of it as a review. We will be presented with our bill, an account of what we owe. "We shall all stand before the judgment seat of Christ," says the apostle (Rom. 14:10). God will present us with our bill. God's own computer will tally the total, and the bill will be huge. You can examine the receipts for yourself, but bickering will be useless. We'll be standing before God, the heavenly accountant, and we will all know—all doubts will be gone—that he is the I AM.

Christ will atone for the believers. He is, after all, himself the judge. He died for us, for our debts, took them all—zillions of them—upon himself.

Those who don't know him won't have an opportunity to acknowledge him. That time is past. Nothing, absolutely nothing, will be in their accounts; and they will hide, but not well, or long. The sentence will be read in each individual conscience.

That sentence is, in a way, hell itself—the worm that restlessly gnaws without ever dying, the fire in the conscience that never dies. No torture could be worse. Eternal punishment is fire within. At that day, God's reality will be front and center. To be banished from the reality of goodness will be eternal torture, and it's something people will recognize with an immediacy and finality that will shrink and decimate forever.

On earth we can pretend to hide from God, shut the curtains, pull the drapes, and lock the door. But Judgment Day will blow the roof off our privacy and slash away all veils and silly facades. The essence of hell is absence from God's holy presence. There is no leaving the vacuum created outside of God's love. When his presence ceases to flood through us, eternal death has come.

All of us need to know God in Christ in this life. After death, this knowledge will hold us fast and put us in company with the very source of love and grace.

But woe to him or her who comes to a knowledge of God only at the judgment. To people who aren't near to him in life, such knowledge will begin eternal torment.

DYING HE
WORSHIPED

By faith Jacob, when he was a dying, blessed both the sons of
Joseph; and worshiped, leaning upon the top of his staff.
—Hebrews 11:21

A person has absolutely no choice about the occasion of his or her birth. When the time comes for a baby to be delivered, the event simply happens. Lacking consciousness, a child is the victim of biological forces far beyond his or her control when the trip down the birth canal begins. No one needs a handbook on being born.

Some of us will have no more control over our deaths than we did over our births. Accidents, heart attacks, or strokes whisk us out of this world quickly and without warning, allowing no opportunity for a person to face death. Some require drugs to be freed from pain so immense it would otherwise terrorize us and our loved ones.

But others will die more slowly and certainly more thoughtfully. And when we do, we should remember that, unlike birth, death is an act. We are not simply passive in the process. We face it, and we act accordingly.

To court death is, of course, flat wrong. Suicide is an act of cowardice in a way, because until the very end the fight to live should continue unabated. But once God calls, once death is at the door, the act of dying can be the occasion for coming near unto God. Perhaps we need more heroic deaths—not in battle, but in spirit.

Jacob's death is the only dying really celebrated in Scripture, but he is, like all the saints in Hebrews 11, a role model. The Bible says he didn't give in to his distress on his deathbed; he didn't break down at leaving loved ones behind. Instead, he gathered his family around him and blessed them, used his last words to do a little holy prophecy, pointing his grandchildren to the kingdom of heaven.

The passage in Hebrews lists Jacob's moment of death as his greatest act of faith. On his deathbed, with his last breaths, Jacob the wrestler conceded that the victories of his life belonged to the Lord. In dying, he worshiped God.

You might not think it true, but those who don't believe in God can go as quietly and easily into death as those who do. In fact, in some ways even believers have come to think that the best way to go is quietly and calmly. But a stoic acceptance of the reality of death isn't an act of worship. Jacob *blessed* his grandkids. Jacob gave them a moral and spiritual lesson. Jacob actually worshiped, readying himself and his family to meet God.

Perhaps we'd do well to take better advantage of the opportunities for real ministry with which death presents us. When the dying are isolated from the living, when drugs suppress consciousness, death ceases to be a preacher of deep seriousness; the Lord of life—and death—is not remembered.

It goes without saying that deathbed prayers carry no excess baggage. As we face God, the trappings of our lives fall away like chaff. Deathbed prayers teach all of us how to pray.

But Jacob did more. He worshiped. In dying, he gave God praise, thanksgiving, and honor, maybe in a fashion more pure and unadulterated than he had offered throughout his entire life. In a way, our deathbed worship summarizes our relationship to God and is a kind of capstone to the worship we gave him throughout our lives. Everything we know and believe is, at that moment, illuminated, enriched, and deepened. God is closer to us than ever before.

When a family like Jacob's sees courageous faith at the end of life, their whole language of faith is enriched. Think of how he must have affected his family when he worshiped with them. He brought his grandkids into the presence of God and made them feel the divine presence closer at hand than ever before. It had to be that way.

Dying can be an occasion of sacred reality, effective to the glory of God in the lives of those who are left behind. This is what it must have been for the family of Jacob.

GIVE YOURSELF TO FASTING AND PRAYER

. . . that ye may give yourselves to fasting and prayer.
—1 Corinthians 7:5

D oes it ever strike you as inconsistent for the church to believe fervently in the authority of Scripture and yet simply skip over all those passages that commend the old practice of fasting? The Old Testament is full of examples of fasting, but then so is the New Testament. Christ himself fasted forty days and forty nights, we're told. What's more he told his disciples that shooing away certain kinds of evil spirits can be accomplished *only* by prayer and fasting (Matt. 17:21).

The early church practiced fasting quite regularly (see Acts 13:2). And we know that the Roman, Greek, and Nestorian churches fasted as well. The Reformers wouldn't have considered *not* fasting. And if you read the diaries of the famous New England Puritan Cotton Mather, you'll find fasting a frequent practice in his personal devotions too.

If both Scripture and history extol fasting as a significant part of a religious life, how is it that fasting is almost nonexistent among today's believers?

Part of our reluctance may be traced to the book of Isaiah: "Is not this the fast that I have chosen?" Isaiah preaches, "to loose the bands of wickedness, to undo the heavy burdens, and let the oppressed go free, and that ye break every yoke?" (58:6). What's behind the prophet's denunciation is tradition gone to sleep, dead formalism. He's not taking on fasting per se; but he is roundly criticizing the meaningless repetition of an action, no matter how pious the appearance.

So let's cut to the quick here. It's not the practice of fasting, but the death of the practice that incurs Isaiah's wrath. Therefore, we practice godliness when we oppose dead formalism—at least that's what is at stake in Isaiah. But fasting itself is appointed of God.

"And this is eternal life, that they might know thee the only true God" (John 17:3). That idea is the theme of everything we've been talking about: that eternity is ours in our nearness to the Father and his nearness to us—not just someday, but now. And how do we best come to him? In prayer. And what is the function of fasting? Simply this, to nourish prayer.

But more. The aim of fasting is not simply to refrain from food. Diets do that. Fasting weakens the life of the body and, at the same time, elevates the life of the soul. Are the two—body and soul—in mortal conflict? Yes and no.

Let's put this bluntly. Eat too much, and you're hardly in an attitude for prayer. Banquets aren't particularly conducive to heartfelt devotions. Busy yourself too much with making money, and the distance between you and the Lord will stretch into miles. It's not easy to be close to God when we're cozy with the world.

Should we, therefore, cloister ourselves, join a monastery? No. Throughout this book we've been talking about myriad ways of coming close to God and experiencing the eternity we all seek in life. Running away from our daily lives is no answer because many of the opportunities we have to know God come in the busy moments of our everyday lives. Give money away to the poor, for instance, and you'll experience something of God.

Believers should take advantage of every opportunity to come near unto God, and one of those, certainly, is fasting. Some may want to fast regularly; some only in times of trial. Don't impose your ways on others. But fasting is a legitimate habit of a believer's life.

If it's done honestly, fasting not only enhances our prayer life, but also leads us away from material extravagance in every part of our lives. It leads us even to fight injustice, in the manner Isaiah preached, because it frees us from self-gratification and forces us to trust in the Creator and Sustainer of the universe. Fasting brings us nearer to God and gives us a taste of eternity.

From time to time, that's not a bad practice.

THAT OUR PRAYER
SHOULD NOT

Thou hast covered thyself with a cloud,
that our prayer should not pass through.
—Lamentations 3:44

Stroll through almost any Christian bookstore and you'll find enough books on prayer to threaten your credit card limit. Everyone, it seems, wants to know how to do it. Tons of us must be mixed up.

Who hasn't sat through public prayers that seemed to rise no higher than the ceiling fan? Who hasn't heard prayers, even in worship, that sounded more like arguments or mini-sermons than real supplication to God? Who hasn't whizzed through a set of words that pass as prayer before a meal or at some special event when, traditionally, someone had to pray? Repitition becomes vain quite easily with us. Sometimes simply the preacher's tone of voice can tune us out.

The Bible insists that not all prayers are equal. Sometimes they're silly chatting, sometimes they're profound and powerful, sometimes they seem almost boring to God: "when ye make many prayers, I will not hear" (Isa. 1:15). Then again, there are times when it seems God isn't accessible: "Thou hast covered thyself with a cloud, that our prayer should not pass through."

This is an almost absurd comparison, but try it on anyway. A child wants, say, a cookie. Does he or she stand up in the middle of the sandbox and yell? (If so, the parent is in real trouble.) Most kids go into the house, find Mom or Dad, and then ask.

And so it should be with prayer. If we want to make our prayers meaningful, we have to find God first. To pray without finding him is little more than public posturing.

On this score the Israelites may have had it much easier. Because they knew exactly where God made his home, when they prayed they quickly turned themselves in that direction as if to face him. They felt they had to look him in the eye.

Today, God doesn't dwell in a some desert tabernacle, but our intent, in some ways, needs to be the same as that of the Israelites. We need to search him out, to look him in the eye, so to speak, before we begin to address him. If we don't, our prayers are peanut shucks. We must come near unto God, be confident in his promises, and trust him to listen; *then* we can pray.

And we do so in Jesus' name because we're powerless in our own. If we think God Almighty will hear our petitions packaged in our human sin, we're wrong. It's only in Christ's name that we can even approach the Father.

What prevents us from attaining a real connection with God? It may well be our sin—something left unconfessed, or something confessed but not yet forgiven. Maybe our thoughts wander or our imaginations are simply too active to allow us to focus on being in God's own presence. Maybe we're unprepared, still ticked at our spouse for some incidental thing that happened a few minutes before. Maybe we've habitually been superficial, taking on public prayer as a badge of our personal righteousness. Saying one's prayers habitually is even less important than brushing one's teeth. Habit means nothing because it leads to nothing. Whatever our problem, there's something thundercloud-like separating us from being heard.

In real prayer, the pray-er comes to understand very well when a cloud passes between her and the face of the Lord; and when it does, she does everything in her power to get rid of it, to bring herself prostrate before the God of her life. And when she does, the real, living, life-infusing connection occurs. The gates of heaven swing open, and prayer passes through, ascending to the face of the Holy One.

It's that simple. If you know there's no contact, then get up off your knees and make contact. Then, once you're connected, get back down. In this very struggle, you blow away the clouds and deal with your own alienation from God. By way of that act, grace in Christ is restored, and he comes close enough for us to speak to him. Then we're ready to pray.

AND TO WHOM-
SOEVER THE SON
WILL REVEAL HIM

No man . . . knoweth the Father, save the Son,
and he to whomsoever the Son will reveal him.
—Matthew 11:27

Who can doubt the words of the psalmist: "The heavens declare the glory of God; and the firmament sheweth his handiwork" (19:1)? Anyone who's ever taken the time to look knows that somewhere in the glorious majesty of a starry night there is something of God Almighty. Beneath an open sky, even an unbeliever has to take pause.

A knowledge of God exists, really, in the malls of our everyday experience. Breathtaking landscapes aren't the only revelation of his might. Something of God is in us—all of us humans. Paul claims that even unbelievers "show the work of the law written in their hearts, their conscience also bearing witness, and their thoughts the meanwhile accusing or else excusing one another" (Rom. 2:15). In the beauty of the lily and the machinations of the human mind, one can spy the reality of God.

But then how do we read this verse? "No man . . . knoweth the Father, save the Son, and he to whomsoever the Son will reveal him"? An apparent contradiction?

The subtlety of difference begs clarification. *Knowledge of God* is accessible all around us and offered to every last human being. *Knowledge of the Father*, however, is the exclusive blessing of those who know him through his Son, Jesus Christ.

As we all know, Satan himself has a knowledge of God. If he didn't know God, he'd have had no sinful reason to rebel against the Lord of the universe. Satan had to know God. He knows him so well, in fact, that

Scripture says that he trembles. Satan's teeth chatter at the reality of God. We, God's children, are comforted by the very same reality because we know him as Father.

Those who know Christ, the Word made flesh, have not only a general knowledge of God but a saving knowledge of his reality. Those who don't believe in Christ don't share that knowledge until they are reconciled in our Savior and thereby come to know God as all believers do—as Father. What Christ tells us is that this saving knowledge of God comes only through him, through his Son, our human link to the Father.

Now, to refine it just a bit, consider this. Knowing that God came to earth in the form of man and that all revelation begins in Christ, the living Word—just knowing that, in the same manner as we know the law of gravity—isn't at all the same phenomenon as knowing God in one's heart. Head knowledge is not the same as heart knowledge. Only those who have been brought near unto God through his Son really *know fully* the truth of the gospel's good news.

We're not just hair-splitting here. Listen to this. Those who really know God, as fully as human beings can, see God even more clearly in a starry night than those who don't. Our nearness to God himself brings his splendid creation to us in technicolor.

So what? you ask. Here's the goods. Sometimes those who are recently converted find such spiritual ecstasy in his presence that they want to sing forever of his majesty, to concentrate their lives' tasks on basking in the glory of Christ. That's commendable, of course, as long as it isn't accomplished at the expense of the beauty of the world he loves.

When we are converted through Christ, we need to let that same light of redemption, that light we know in our inner life, shine gloriously on our outer life as well. "In the beginning was the Word, and the Word was with God, and the Word was God" (John 1:1). Those familiar words insist that Christ shines not only in us, but in his world as well.

Don't run away from the world—that's the idea. Live gloriously in a creation that is immensely brightened by your knowledge of God. What's important to remember is that everything we see around us looks different as a result of our knowledge of the Father through his Son. Our knowing God—in head and heart—unites the life of grace with the life of nature in a glorious harmony and turns the whole world—all of history and science and art, everything we are and shall be—into . . . you guessed it . . . into one mighty revelation of the Father. Wow! Don't miss it.

CONTINUALLY
WITH THEE

Nevertheless I am continually with thee.
—Psalm 73:23

Those of us who take subways or buses to work know firsthand the oddity of traveling daily with some people, seeing them for years, even knowing their reading habits, but never really coming close to them at all, even though a significant part of our everyday lives takes place only an elbow away.

On the other hand, most of us also know how, when separated physically from those we love, they still appear constantly in our imaginations. New lovers obsess sometimes, don't they? In the hours they are apart, they're really never parted at all. Even when they're away from each other, they're intimate in some way, sometimes sickeningly so.

It's wonderful to reach out and touch someone, but proximity isn't a prerequisite to intimacy. Two souls a continent apart can be closer to each other than some roommates.

What's clear, however, is that any fellowship of the soul demands fellowship of the body, for we are one creature, after all. Part of the joy of eternal glory is the prospect of reuniting with loved ones lost, loved ones who we'll see once again in glorified bodies.

But we're made with such intimate complexity that the body itself is not required for close fellowship. Even when apart, we can be close. How many times haven't grieving parents tearfully whispered over the bodies of their children that those departed ones will never, ever leave them fully. Ask a parent who has lost a child. Those kids never are completely gone.

When Asaph says, "Nevertheless I am continually with thee," the only way for us to understand that testimony is in a spiritual sense. We can never really be absent from God. He's in every throb of our blood and quiver of our nerves. He's always beside us.

But once again, that he is there doesn't mean we know him fully. God must, after all, approach us; and we, responding, have to open ourselves to him. That's the process.

How does it begin? In joy, in sorrow, in pain, in grief; in extreme moments in our lives, almost all of us feel God knocking at the door. He comes richly into our deepest moments, and when he does, we must respond, because those moments, fraught with whatever emotion, are deeply precious and full of opportunity for life eternal.

The word used in this verse is *continually*, not *continuously*. There is a difference. *Continually* means always; *continuously* means from time to time. What Asaph wants, quite frankly, is *to walk with God always*. It's that simple.

But that doesn't mean that he wants to live his life in deep and full-throated meditation, no matter how holy. He doesn't propose to lose himself in divine mysticism. All of that is okay, but that's not what is intended. If it were, then we should live in monasteries, where all our waking hours could be spent in study and chants.

But to be near unto God means living robustly in his grace, so that his nearness permeates our feelings, our sensations, our thinking, our imagining, our wills, our acts, and every last word that comes from our hearts and mouths. Our love for God is unique because his love, as obsessed as we can be with him, does not distract us from the world. Instead, it sends us out into it, full of heavenly vision and burgeoning thanksgiving.

In all time and all things, our thanks rises from our acts in this world. We give him, for his rich gifts, our lives. Our eternal joy is what we do with our time. It is the Lord who brings us to every moment of our lives, and we offer those moments back to him in praise.

Like nothing else, Asaph wanted to be continually with God because he knew, as all of us do, what it meant to be estranged. In fact, he knew estrangement so well that he wanted no part of it anymore. He wanted to be with his Lord.

That's the mark of believers. They know what joy there is in being near unto God, and they want nothing else. Those who truly believe bring Christ into everything they do because he is always with them.

I HIDE ME
WITH THEE

I flee unto thee to hide me.
—Psalm 143:9

Let's return to the barnyard. Yellow balls of fluff scurry everywhere, pecking in the dust, while their mother casts a wary eye about, on the lookout for trouble. The moment she sees something, she gathers them under her wings, even if they don't want to go. In fact, only when they see whatever the danger is—maybe a chicken hawk—do they take off to her for protection. But when they do, they throw themselves totally into her care.

Inevitably in life we face chicken hawks. Don't we wish that weren't so? Inevitably times come when all we can do is take off to the Lord for the protection beneath his motherly wings. No one is immune from times of severe crisis, no matter how sanctified his or her walk with God. Storms rage. Terminal disease comes even to health-food addicts. Death strikes wherever humans draw breath. But in every crisis, the Lord offers his protection, asking us to respond.

Human beings answer that call in different ways. In the lashing winds of a hurricane, for instance, some who don't know God might cry "Lord, Lord" in a voice that gets lost in the tumult. A door away, the neighbor will be so busy trying to save his own life that he never even thinks about God. Down the street, others may hear the voice of the Lord in the terrifying rush of the wind, but not raise their voices to him in prayer. But on the next block, someone will hear God's call and find protection under his wings.

We are talking here about extremities, worst-case scenarios. Hiding in God is something other than walking by his side. For one thing, it's temporary. Storms pass, danger diminishes, intruders leave, death occurs finally. Life is rife with upsetting circumstances, but not every crisis demands that kind of desperate hiding. But when we're up to our ears in horror, when the floodwaters threaten every last thing we own and even our families, then we run. We literally *hide* in God.

When we do, we carry no plan of attack and care little for anything with our name on it. We abandon ourselves, so to speak, and give our destinies to the Lord. In fact, it's a kind of despair about ourselves that prompts our hiding. We know very well that we're unable to do anything at all about our fate, so we cast our souls on the God who made us. If it's possible to talk about *despair* and *faith* in the same context, then *despair* is the right word, for hiding in God demands an abandonment of self. David says earlier in this psalm that his own heart was desolate, unable to find a way through distress (143:4).

Believers can find refuge from even the unspeakable agonies of terminal disease; they still may hold out against death because they find refuge beneath the wings of God. Huge family problems, consuming grief, endless adversity, desperate poverty, vicious personal attacks—even though these problems may not have their source in one's faith, they deeply affect our relationship to God. They make war against our strength, and, for the believer anyway, our strength lies in the Lord.

There is a process here worth noting. When dire adversity strikes, we begin, in faith, to resist those forces that threaten to undo us; we try to fight off the storm until our strength falters. But then, when our strength is depleted, we put forth the one last heroic effort, the act that triumphs: we let go of ourselves and let God cover us with his wings. At that moment, no matter how tempest-tossed, the believer hides himself with God, and God binds up our wounds and gently heals.

Hiding in Christ means having listened to his voice; and, having listened, responding in an act of desperate faith. You can bet that right now, somewhere near you, it's happening.

Thou Dost Not
Answer Me

I cry unto thee, and thou dost not hear me.
—Job 30:20

One rule of thumb about real prayer is that it's not just empty words. Real prayers expect real answers. They face God straight on and wait for a reply.

Not all prayers are equal. Formal prayers, for instance, are much different than those offered up in the silence of our privacy. They are occasional, and they wear a public face. But are they therefore bad? No. Formal prayers preserve the habit. Formal prayers, as defective as some may be, at least keep us in touch and keep us praying. As long as we keep praying, at some point our lifelessness will ignite with spiritual energy, sparkling with intensity and faith.

If true prayer truly expects answers, then what kind of answers do we expect? Nowadays most of us expect a word to the soul, an impression the Holy Spirit accomplishes. There was a time when people expected the visitation of angels or some spiritual vision. But today we usually await being surprised by the comfort of God.

Worship isn't prayer exactly, but it's a relative. We want our worship to be pleasing to the Almighty, like our prayers. And we expect at least this much, that we will receive the satisfaction of knowing that what we brought to God was good and pleasant in his eyes.

Not all worship is. The story of Cain and Abel, even though the medium is sacrifice, is a vivid reminder that not everything we aim towards God Almighty is greeted with equal appreciation. Cain offered good meat, but what he did stunk in God's nostrils. The Lord God Almighty is under no obligation to commend our efforts to worship him.

But we're talking about silence here. For the believer, God's silence is more painful and greviously hard to take than any experience in life. Job's complaints of unanswered prayer, "Thou dost not hear me," have an echo in the psalmist's abject misery: "My God, my God, why hast thou forsaken me? . . . O my God, I cry in the daytime, but thou hearest me not" (22:1-2). Even Jesus felt the torture of God's silence.

So don't get down on yourself if your prayers aren't answered. While our sin may be the reason for some of the silence that answers us, Christ Almighty can't be blamed for his unanswered prayer. Our lack of faith is not always the cause for God's silence; the greatest biblical saints felt that silence too. Take some comfort here: if your most earnest prayers are not answered, you're in pretty good company. You don't have to blame yourself. What all those prayers illustrate is that sometimes God *intentionally* doesn't answer. He's got his reasons.

But think about the Lord's Prayer. Our needs—*our* daily bread, *our* forgiveness—these begin only halfway through. What comes first is adoration. All too often when we pray, we begin with what we think God can do for us. That's pure arrogance, isn't it? That's putting ourselves first. That's not recognizing that God sees so much more than we do. The misery of our soul's punyness is that, even in earnest prayer, we're nowhere near the sacred height of God, who sees a whole world more widely than we do. He knows the entire landscape.

Don't let your soul grow faint in the silence of unanswered prayer, for know this: God is dealing with those he loves in his own way. Our experience teaches us that answers sometime miraculously arrive without our asking, often enough in strange packages we never anticipated. The point needs to be restated: why should we be spared the very feelings God allowed his Son to experience?

Sometimes absence makes the love grow fonder. We know that. God knows that. His silence may well be his way of fortifying our faith, of sanctifying us, his way of telling us more about ourselves than we know.

Why the silence? To prepare us for a glorious future. That's the point here. By drawing a cloud between us and his voice, he may well be leading us, by his silence, to a higher and richer enjoyment of life with him forever.

THE COURSES OF
THE AGE ARE HIS

His ways are eternal.
—Habakkuk 3:6
(translation from the Dutch version)

O ld Year's Eve and New Year's Day are peculiar, aren't they? Because we come to the end of the calendar, we quite naturally pause and reflect on both what's behind and what we believe is to come. Every year there are 365 rotations of the earth, but only once do we step out of ourselves and take note of time.

The Creator inhabits a wholly different world than we do. His ways are eternal. He feels the need for no New Year's resolutions, no "Auld Lang Syne." The I AM bathes himself in eternity. Even though none of us can quite understand what *eternity* means, it's fatal for us to forget that fundamental difference between ourselves and God.

The fact is, he sets the clocks of our lives. He gives us seconds and minutes and hours; he puts the calendars on our walls. The rotation of the earth, the pulse of blood through our arteries, the aging process of our skin—all of it is God-designed. We didn't invent time, but it is our bathwater—and it's wholly different than eternity.

New Year's can be a blessing. Even if only once a year, we can grab the opportunity to look back and forward through time. That ability to step outside ourselves, however clumsily, is a privilege, isn't it? We aren't just creatures of the clock; we can, at least, watch it turn.

But time itself is only a convenience. It isn't real. Time is God-chopped eternity; it's little divisable chunks, chopped up for us. God didn't need it. It's a gimmick he invented for us, and it's not real, not at all.

What's real is eternity—really. What matters, finally, is not time but our destiny; and our destiny is eternal. It's incredibly easy to forget that, isn't it? But let's just push the idea a little further.

In God's eyes, a year doesn't mean anything. In God's eyes, our lives are not plotted by months, or days, or years, or even by lifetimes. The plan for our lives didn't begin with us, nor even with our parents and grandparents and great-grandparents. It began in eternity. What's seventy years to the whole destiny of humankind? Piddly.

What's more, our destiny doesn't end with our deaths. We stop breathing, but we don't just end. Our lifetime is only a kind of diving board, right? We gain eternity.

People who don't understand that get frustrated easily, especially at year's end. The only way a single year has any meaning is in a much larger context, a much larger plan—and the author of that plan is our God. Now, given that fact, of what importance is temporary joy? Once we start to believe that it's this, that, or the other thing that we really need—even in our devotion to God—we're falling into the worst of our finiteness. Our joys this year are part of a larger diagram; so are our tears. Remember that in your distress.

We'll be frustrated and gloomy if all we ever see is the next two or three yards on the pilgrimage we take through life. We'll miss the courage given to those with a larger faith; we'll miss the inspiration to see our destinies; we'll miss the joy we have in knowing that God's hand operates infinitely and fully in our living *and* our dying.

Those who judge happiness on the basis of what they have, or get, or can control are going to discover that what they're after is unadulterated dust. One of God's greatest gifts to us is explained in Ecclesiastes 3: "He has set eternity in our hearts" (NIV). He created us—now listen to this!—with the capacity to lift ourselves up from what's around us and latch onto the eternal. We can do it.

With that gift—eternity in our hearts—we can face everything that comes along, because we'll know, deeply and securely, that whatever happens to us, whatever heartaches we suffer, whatever joys are ours, there's a purpose and destiny for our lives. It's a destiny designed expressly for us by none other than God Almighty.

PRAISE HIM UPON THE STRINGS

Praise him with the timbrel and dance: praise him with
stringed instruments and organs.
—Psalm 150:4

When the curmudgeon-like American journalist H. L. Mencken defined Puritanism as "the haunting fear that someone, somewhere might be happy," he might well have included more believers than America's Puritan ancestors. It's not hard for Christians to be dour. After all, we're commanded to sobriety and purity, warned against all kinds of cockiness, and exhorted to be wary of money. That such believers might seem austere, forbidding, and darkened with worry is not hard to believe.

But the Bible holds nothing back in its relentless command to praise. The Holy Spirit drives us to worship, to cultivate nearness, to celebrate God's astonishing reality. So energized does the psalmist get in his outburst of joy that he directs the angels to join in the party: "Bless ye the Lord, all ye his hosts; ye ministers of his, that do his pleasure" (103:21).

And that's not even enough. In his fit of delirious delight, he realizes that breathing things alone can't make a big enough sound, so he begs inanimate creation to join the great choir: "Praise him . . . all ye stars of light . . . snow, and vapors; stormy winds" (Ps. 148:3, 8) and "O Lord, our Lord, how excellent is thy name in all the earth" (Ps. 8:1). Listen, as every last language on earth blesses God's name.

Music is absolutely integral to creation. Anyone who's ever heard a mountain stream knows nature's song. Birds may well be nature's finest soloists, but the wind through the willows can sing God's praise just as beautifully. A gentle rain makes a great contralto, and if you listen just right, a whole city can become a symphony. Nothing is as gifted in performance, however, as the human voice, capable as it is of so much sound in so many variations.

It's sound that we're talking about here, sound specifically designed to bring praise. What does it matter whether it's produced by striking metal, causing tight strings to vibrate, or by pushing one's own breath through tubes and valves—sound is always a motion that rises from an impulse in the soul.

God is the real artist, of course. Sound was there before a human ear was created, before Adam and Eve heard joyful noise from the branches of Eden's trees. What a blessing it is for us, his children, to be able to bring him praise in sound, in harmony, in music from a thousand different instruments, each with its own peculiar flavor.

The magic of music is that in its harmonies it carries the very voice of the soul. The undulation and motion of the heart flows out in music, no matter what the medium. In chorus or orchestra, it's enriched by the very phenomenon that produces it individually, as together God's people, playing with each other's own musical testimonies, harmonize their soul's utterings in one mighty stream of adoration.

In its harmonies of soul and body, music moves even the listener to love. Even the angels join in the heavenly chorus. World cultures produce myriad styles, all of them designed for the same purpose. An oboe, a bass viol, a horn taken from an animal's head, and a reed pulled from a swamp—alone, they're interesting; together, they're music.

It's not pure, of course, and it won't be until we reach glory; and when musicians aim at less than God's glory, they cheapen what they do. Cacophony, often enough, results. Music has a higher aim than simply pleasing the ear or creating misguided emotion; the purpose of the human voice, of vibrating strings, of brass and cymbal, is to witness to God's goodness. Where the purpose is less than that, God's people sense something wrong. Music has tremendous influence for good and evil. Bad music counts its victims by thousands. We should be wary.

Any time sacred music revives in a culture, good things are at work. A nation that doesn't sing and make music to the glory of the Lord enfeebles itself.

Let all creation praise his name!

IN SALEM IS
HIS TABERNACLE

In Salem also is his tabernacle, and his dwelling place in Zion.
—Psalm 76:2

Some mysteries are simply too divine to unravel. Like this one. If we believe the Old Testament, then we must buy the absurd proposition that the Lord God Almighty once had a street address. Not just once either. Throughout the Israelites' forty-year sojourn, the Levites set up the tabernacle along a number of trails. Only when they came to Canaan did the tabernacle stay at Jerusalem.

How can the I AM be simultaneously all over and only in one place? That's the tough question. For if indeed he once lived on Mt. Zion, then at least back then he could have been nowhere near, say Scotland, could he? How could we call him omnipresent?

What's at issue here is God's infinite nature and our lack of the same. There's simply no way our finite minds can understand and appreciate his infinity. It's beyond us.

But human beings have long tried to bridge that gap. For centuries we pulled clay up from beneath our feet and tried to make infinity from plain old dirt. Millions have tried to sculpt brass or stone or plaster into the shape of what is, by its essence, shapeless. Needless to say, idolatry has never worked.

Only God can do it—and he did, for us. He began in the desert by reversing humanity's attempts at idolatry. You remember that he specifically barred from his temple every form of idol. What's more, by directing his people to only one address, he centralized worship, all the while insisting that he was a spirit, not an object. He began to bring the infinite to us, his very finite creatures.

But when the temple idea had run its course and more was required, he gave us a new temple in the form of his incarnated Word—Jesus Christ, the God who came to earth; and then, once Christ had ascended, he gave us his Holy Spirit, whose interior designs in our hearts make us each the dwelling place of God. Incredibly, the infinite has come to live in the finite.

Jesus Christ was and is God. He dwells with the Father; but he also dwells with us. Through the Spirit, he takes up habitation in each of his believers and makes us his temples. He dwells at our address.

Thus, the bridge between the finite (us) and the infinite (God) is laid by God himself. He started the process of our redemption, but that process doesn't end with us or in us; rather it ends once again with him as he fashions our lives, his dwelling place, to his own praise and honor. Even though it's mostly his job, his work is our blessing; we come to know that our contact with God comes through Christ, that through communion of the saints we can appreciate God's fellowship, and that the Holy Ghost, doing his work within us, fashions his dwelling place. We know something of his infinity, even in our finiteness.

That sounds so theoretical, doesn't it? Of course, there's more. We all know our fellowship with God becomes more real in those moments when we touch other human beings, when we know them most personally. The deepest fellowship we can have is no coffee break. It's the sacrament of communion, our shared testimony to the glory of Christ. No higher and holier institution has been given to humankind than when in the night in which he was betrayed, Christ broke the bread and poured the wine and called his Holy Supper into being.

Communion is the confluence of all the lines that create our fellowship with God. It's our point of contact, and it's offered only in the body of believers.

Let's cut to the chase. Nothing is more heinous than the act of breaking the fellowship of believers. When people, by their dissension and their passionate contention for the right of their own particular views, cause this fellowship of God's saints to weaken and grow faint, they chip away at Salem, at the very address of God's infinite nature.

That person who uses the church for his or her own ends, who breaks the communion of the saints to propagate his or her own views, does something monstrous by demolishing something the Lord Almighty so lovingly constructed for us.

THE NIGHT IS
FAR SPENT

The night is far spent, the day is at hand.
—Romans 13:12

Dawn creeps in stealthily from the east. Already an hour before the appearance of the sun, a mysterious glow rises from the horizon until the entire canopy of sky seems backlit. Intensity heightens in the east as grays dissolve into whites, and the sun itself, brighter than an orange in winter, peeks from a landscape drenched in gold.

There's a process to the day. We don't move from night to noon as if someone had flipped a switch. It's almost embarrassing to think about, isn't it—that kind of radical change? Every day we'd walk into life with sleep lines creasing our faces. Instead, the world is lit by a divine rheostat that gently and smoothly brightens the stage, each day, for our lives.

In some ways, our lives after conversion exist in a slowly rising dawn. The big day, the brightest day, comes only when the glory of Christ breaks over us. Up until that day, it's true that we walk in the light. But it's only half bright.

That is as true today as it was in the day of the apostle Paul, when conversions had to have been even more radical than they are today. Speaking for himself and for the converts at Rome, he says, "now [even though it's years after their conversions] it is high time to awake out of this sleep [their condition, even though they're converted]....The night is far spent, the day is at hand" (Rom. 13:11-12).

The light of God's reality comes into us and affects us in three stages. First, it brightens us inwardly; our inner selves stretch and grow. Then second, in response, we begin to act on that renewed inner strength. We become more animated as the day brightens, and we gain a much clearer sense of how we can grasp a foothold in the world. Our steps become firm, and we develop morally.

The third step is not so much a turning inward as a turning upward. What happens is that our intimacy with God himself increases as we bathe ever more comfortably in his light. We're aware of the darkness all around us, and we still feel uncertainty, anxiety, and suspicion as we try to find our way. But through a closer walk with God, through our nearness to him, and by the light of his countenance, we feel his intimacy and tenderness.

Like the dawn, however, these stages emerge slowly and not always visibly. Just as there is no switch for the day, no one pulls a cord and—just like that—becomes a mature, sanctified Christian. Those who think they do are kidding themselves.

Even though the light we observe now in our renewed lives, our illumined lives, doesn't reach the brightness we will know someday, that light still turns our narrow paths into freeways. It enriches human existence in all ways because it discloses to us the route we take to come to God. Everything looks more beautiful in the light of the Son.

As our fellowship with the Lord increases, we experience a walk with God which those who don't know the Lord don't begin to understand. And while some among the converted don't really grow in their knowledge of God, don't experience his peace, many certainly do.

Those who know God's light as richly as we can know it in this half-lit world know absolutely nothing of standing still. By growing in their Christian walk, they enter more fully into the secrets of the infinite. When they awake in the morning, they do so in God's light, a light they carry with them every hour of the day, no matter where they work.

Who are these people? The salt of the salt, really. What's more, they are the salt of God's church. You know them too.

These people are truly gifts to us. They're sanctified saints who preserve his church from desecration and dissolution. They're like planets. They reflect the brilliance of divine light. They shine in the darkness of the world. Thank God.

WITHOUT GOD
IN THE WORLD

*At that time ye were without Christ, being aliens from the
commonwealth of Israel, and strangers from the covenants of
promise, having no hope, and without God in the world.*
—Ephesians 2:12

Today atheism is not only commonplace, in some quarters it's fashionable. Those who deny God are far more numerous now than they were years ago, and in many cases no one bugs them for what they preach. Today, believers don't shudder at the atheists' rhetoric as they used to either, and that indifference creates a problem.

Think of it this way. When for the very first time a child hears something bad about his or her parents, the initial reaction is defensiveness. But when that child hears negative things time and time again, her reaction goes numb. We take such criticism more calmly and suffer thereby a real moral loss.

Or how about this. When our political leaders are constantly criticized in the press, in talk shows, on late-night television, we get accustomed to hearing bad things about them. We stop reacting negatively, and our leaders gradually lose credibility in our eyes. What's more—and what's worse—as the poison works within us, it extinguishes our own aspiration for public service. It's insidious really, isn't it?

Yet it goes on. And so does a relentless campaign against God in our culture.

It is undeniable that a serious menace to public life exists when some of our culture's most prominent figures make religion laughable. Even the heathen understood the danger in forsaking religion. But the poison is in us, in our culture, and we seem powerless to do anything about it.

Empires leave track records behind them, and many of those histories look identical. A nation and a culture is born and soon grows wealthy. Wealth leads to moral decay, moral decay to religious indifference, religious indifference to atheism—a world without God—and atheism to ruin.

Paul knew that. In fact, that's what he told the Ephesian Christians. He said they once lived in a time when the world was without God. But no more.

What happens to well-intentioned people is that they begin to use religion as if it were health food. They think faith important on a few holidays and for a marriage ceremony. In fact, they may take the kids to Sunday school because they think children need a good dose of religion, like cod liver oil. Some intelligent (and arrogant) people like to think that religion is good treatment for the masses; it keeps them in line. But atheism springs from indifference.

Often those who deny God love art, practice philanthropy, and promote education enthusiastically. Often they dote on ideals that awaken poetic talent within them. They're nice people. But religion, to them, is superfluous.

How do we reach those people? As important as the creeds and practices of faith—preaching, baptism, holy communion—are, the only way to reawaken a thirst for God in these people is the power of love. Love alone can work salvation. At Ephesus, people who lived in a world without God came to Christ in droves—not by reproach or harsh judgments, but through the love the apostles shouldered selflessly into their lives. Why? In that love, the reality of a life in God is shown clearly. That love thaws frozen hearts.

Look! We have to live in the world; only at death are we called away to another existence. Here, so much works against our faith: wealth, temptation, our work, our recreation, our troubles, and our sorrows. Our busyness distracts us all too often, so that people, even believers, can go on day after day without really thinking about God.

But in the conflict we all face between divided loyalties, only God can equip us with the energy and the armaments to continue to live wholly in his light. We can be real believers only when we stay near unto God, when we live with him, in his Spirit—not apart from the world, but in the very center of our busyness.

We carry his love into all of life, even to the atheists among us, when our nearness to him becomes our own, regenerated, second nature. ❖

I WILL WALK
AMONG YOU

And I will walk among you, and will
be your God, and ye shall be my people.
—Leviticus 26:12

O ne's walk with God is not simply personal. It is personal, certainly, but it is not only personal. If we are to come near unto
God, if we are to be strengthened day by day, then we need to walk closely
with him always, not simply in Sunday worship, morning devotions, or
evening prayers.

If you know a deep and abiding communion with God personally, then
you are, certainly, a believer. If you know this communion within the context of your family life, your family is certainly blessed. If it's true in your
church, then your church is a wonderful place. If it's true in your work-
place, then going to work can never be a chore. Knowing God in every
area of your life brings peace and only more faith.

But don't ever think that walking with God means you've jettisoned sin
from your soul. That doesn't happen, not to the best of us. Sadly, it's possible to walk with God in a way that's still crippled by sin. Most of us
know people who spent most of their lives together—in a marriage or a
business relationship—and always felt contrary toward each other. That
also happens to believers in their walk with God.

We feel this ache for something we shouldn't have—maybe it's someone other than our spouse. But we know terrifyingly well that we can't
have that person. Why? Because God's voice—as he walks with us—is a
bullhorn. So we don't do what we desire, but we grow resentful because we

can't. At ourselves, for our sin? Of course not—at God, for restraining us from whatever it is—money, sex, power, whatever.

It doesn't matter what. If we feel a leash tugging at our necks, we resent the person jerking it. No one knows our resentment better than God, so he becomes angry with us. And therefore we walk with God in a bitterness that isn't at all comforting and nowhere near holy. The whole relationship antagonizes the Holy Spirit.

Oddly enough, those who don't walk with God don't sin in this fashion at all because they don't grieve the Holy Spirit in the same way. But if you're a believer, your antipathy toward God generates its own species of iniquity, something that affects not only your personal life but all your relationships and all of your life.

What's deceptive to others is that the point of the breakdown between God and the believer in a situation like this is often just one problem. In every other way, in every other action, from all points of view, the believer may well look like a saint. But in one miserably, rotten area—many times unseen by others until too late—desire wrestles us to the ground, makes God's presence an irritant, and really comes to make our walk with God something of a nuisance. When that point of sin breaks out into the open, other believers are mystified that such an otherwise good person could take such a free fall. But what we must remember is that God does not sit by idly when his presence becomes an irritant to us. He is angered. He'll walk away.

The command to remember is to follow God in all things, for his paths lead to heaven and his glory. What are his ways? How do we distinguish them from our own? Just keep praying the Lord's Prayer: "Hallowed be thy name. Thy kingdom come. Thy will be done." If your repetition of those words is not vain and meaningless, then God's way of life will begin to become yours. You will feel yourself but a drop of water in surf that rises continuously to his glory.

But a drop of water does not a wave make. His will for our lives always includes our lives with others. Only one human being ever had to walk alone. The rest of us can find fellowship, in fact must find fellowship, if we are to know his way.

Our lives are truly blessed when we walk with God every hour of the day. Then, and only then, will he walk among us.

CLEAVING UNTO HIM

Thou shalt cleave unto the LORD thy God.
—Deuteronomy 30:20

(translation from the Dutch version)

"Cleaving" is a somewhat unusual word today. It defines a relationship that is almost antithetical to individualism. When people think of themselves as strong and powerful, they would rather not admit that cleaving is something good, because cleaving means really, really, really needing someone, more than any of us would like to admit.

Perhaps the best picture of cleaving is a nursing mother and her baby. No husband can cut in on that relationship. When a baby is nursing, the child is more than just happy. The child is not only being fed, but also nourished in love to the point where he or she actually cherishes the warmth of Mom. The moment Mom leaves, the baby cries. That's cleaving.

Anyone reading these words has long ago put babyhood behind. Yet, according to the Bible, God commands us—fully grown, mature, independent human beings, capable of mature and rational decision-making—to cleave unto him with the intensity that a baby cleaves to his mother. Almost repulsive, isn't it?

Also, millions die each day without ever having received word: "Thou shalt cleave unto the Lord thy God." In every country and every continent, people of all ages go to the grave without ever having understood that cleaving is precisely what the Lord wants of all of his people. They've never heard the gospel.

Millions have heard and just simply not paid attention. In Western countries at least, one would be hard-pressed to find a town or city where no church offers baptism or the Lord's Supper. Yet, millions don't take that commandment seriously.

Oh, there are certain times when people do take it seriously. Once in a while revival occurs, and an entire culture is swept up into religious enthusiasm. But then, always, what began as a fervent attempt to come near unto God ends in formalism, factionalism, and dead orthodoxy.

All of us, no matter how saintly we might think ourselves, need to hear this commandment: thou shalt cleave unto the Lord thy God. In fact, those who we might judge most saintly would likely be the first to admit that they too need to be reminded of what God commands. Nobody on this side of death truly cleaves to God.

Cleaving demands understanding intellectually as much as we can of God; but that's not all. Cleaving demands confession of the name of the Lord, but that's not all. Cleaving means we live a holy life full of good works, but that's not all. Cleaving means practicing one's faith by going to church, but that's not enough either. Those who cleave unto God do his will, certainly; but if our actions are generated by anything other than love, those actions create a din worse than cheap cymbals.

Real intimacy with God—real cleaving—took place in Paradise, and it will take place again in the life hereafter. That's it. Only then.

So should we just throw in the towel? It seems silly to pursue true godliness.

Nonsense. Even though we will never know the kind of intimacy now that we will experience in the life to come, we should be hunting for God daily. In every moment and in every way, we should seek him—to worship him, to bring him glory. Our spiritual highs will become more frequent if seeking him is our foremost quest.

Sanctification is a process. With vigilance, coming nearer to him is something that can be learned. In a way, we need to shepherd ourselves. And even though it will never be complete in this vale of tears, we can find more and more space for God in the pattern of daily existence when we continually seek him.

Then Asaph's testimony can be ours: "As for me, it is good to be near unto God." That can be our song, too, piped from the chambers of a heart reconciled to the Lord.

SAMUEL DID NOT
YET KNOW THE LORD

Now Samuel did not yet know the LORD,
neither was the word of the LORD yet revealed to him.
—1 Samuel 3:7

I t's fair to say that all of us know a lot of people. Most of us have no problem recognizing members of our church or workforce when we meet them on the street because we know them—by their faces, their ways of walking, even their bald spots. We know them because we can differentiate them from others.

We know other people in a more intimate way—by character. When students ask teachers for recommendations, they aren't requesting a description of their chin line. What future employers want is a good recommendation from those who know the student well enough to understand what makes the kid tick. That's "inside" knowledge, a sense of heart and will.

The delightful story from Samuel's childhood—his rising three times in response to a voice he mistakenly identified as Eli's—shows very clearly that the boy couldn't differentiate the voice of the Divine Being from that of the old man of the temple. What he needed, at first anyway, was simply the knowledge to enable him to hear God's voice and identify it as such. Three times he went to Eli's bedside, and only when the old man suggested the voice might be from God did a light go on in the boy's mind.

We shouldn't make little Samuel into a dolt. Every one of us has his or her own voice. There are no clones, no copies. That little Samuel didn't know God's voice is understandable, given how many voices make sound waves all around us each day.

But the Lord does have his own voice, and it's our job—like Samuel's—to distinguish it from the sound bites we accumulate from a thousand others. That job may well have been easier for the patriarchs and the apostles, who knew God from special revelation. God actually spoke to many of them. Of course, God actually speaks to us today too, but the voice comes out of Scripture. For us, the Word is the voice of God. It's just as rich, just as full, just as tonally beautiful but, from our point of view, may be less spectacular.

Which is not to say that today no one ever sees visions or dreams dreams in which God's actual voice can be heard. It's foolish to say such things don't happen. But we do know this: those revelations aren't essential to THE WORD. The Bible's writing is finished, over. Anyone who wants to submit another chapter is a victim of sickly mysticism. God's voice is in the Word.

Some people read the Bible for a living and never hear God speaking to them. Some learned big chunks of it by heart as children, and yet it's little more to them than the ditties on greeting cards. Some of them call themselves Christians because they presume Christianity has strong moral power. They think of themselves as good people because they don't break commandments. But they don't know God.

Others don't hear the voice of God but would like to. These people, real searchers, are the quarry God wants. In his employ, we can help in these people's lives in special ways. How? First, by dispensing special treatment. It's interesting how personal Christ was—as was John the Baptist—in his ministering to others. Those who search for God are special-needs people; they require our personal attention.

But woe unto us if our words are only words. What attracts those who seek God is their seeing the sacred power of love in our lives. If they don't see it, we actually hold them back from hearing the voice of God and knowing him.

Remember Eli? His sons, Hophni and Phineas, abused sacred things because their father, the priest, lacked moral courage to be the father he should have been. To enable real seekers to hear God's voice and to know him intimately, God desires our participation, our lives, our commitments. But to do that, we must, very simply, practice what we preach.

THEY MAKE
IT A WELL

Who passing through the valley of Baca
make it a well; the rain also filleth the pools.
—Psalms 84:6

N eed a drink? Walk to the kitchen, turn on the faucet, and there's water. Hard day out on the trail? Your choice: shower or bath. Spilled ketchup on your new white blouse? The washing machine is in the back hall. From all corners of our habitation, we get water. Most houses likely have a dozen spigots, some of them outside for flowers and lawns. Who needs water? There's plenty.

So it's difficult for us to imagine the depth of passion that thirst can actually bring. Human beings die from thirst much more quickly than they die of hunger because water is more immediately essential to life. But how many of us know thirst? Very few.

That's why it's easy to read Scripture's frequent references to God and Christ as a fountain and simply go on, as if the verse had no more meaning than an extra prepositional phrase. Besides, for most of us, a fountain is something in a park—something ceremonial, lit up by floodlights at night, a memorial for fallen war dead or some famous political figure. God is not ceremonial.

When the Bible claims we "thirst after righteousness" or "thirst after the living God," it implies a depth of desire that can be deadly if it's not quenched by the fountain. The tongue sticks to the parched roof of the mouth, making it difficult to speak. The throat dries into sawdust, making words impossible. Water becomes a passion so deep it makes humans do unspeakable things.

How many of us thirst after God with a passion? How many of us can empathize with the writers' passions: "Ho, everyone that thirsteth, come ye to the waters" (Isa. 55:1), and "Whosoever drinketh of the water that I shall give him shall never thirst" (John 4:14)?

The point at which to begin understanding God and his Son as the "fountain of life" is in ancient mountainous villages, where the village spring was in the public square. Everyone came toting baskets and jars, needing water. The whole village drank from a single well, even the horses and cattle. Uncomfortable as it may seem to us, the village fountain was the place where cleanliness appeared and thirst was satisfied, the center of business and commerce, as well as the social hub of community life.

God is that kind of fountain.

My, how things have changed for most of us. Today no one goes downtown for water, unless you buy it purified. Running water is no luxurious feature of a new home; it's a given. Water has come, in a way, to live with us.

As we've said before, in the Old Testament world God had an address; today he's all over the globe. Today, through the Word made flesh, his Spirit has come to make us his tabernacles. Today we don't pilgrimage to the public square, jugs on head; today the living water flows in us.

But even though it's here, we need to open the spigot. Like the water that runs through the pipes in our homes, Christ is always there, waiting. But living water must be put into action. We have to tap it. Our faith must be put into action. The fascinating twist on the verse above is that it says those pilgrims passing through the Valley of Baca "make it a well." In other words, they make the living water a source of renewal and replenishment. They do their faith.

But let's go back two hundred years to the village well at the heart of the community. Some people from the place get rich and decide to build their own source of life. They dig a well for their own personal use. They no longer need the communal fountain. They satisfy their thirst from their own fountains.

Now listen to this: blessed are the poor in spirit, for they still go to the fountain of life. Theirs, we are told, is the kingdom of God (Matt. 5:3).

By My God I Leap
over a Wall

And by my God have I leaped over a wall.
—Psalm 18:29

Imagine Adam and Eve in the garden, apple cores scattered at their feet. Naked as jay birds, they suddenly feel exposed not only to each other but also to every force of nature. For the first time, lions growl, hyenas show their fangs, and snakes rattle, poised to strike. Winds begin to blow cold and fierce, as the sun hides behind clouds. The earth shakes beneath their feet. Creation has suddenly turned against them.

There is no rescue squad, no furnace, no medical clinic, no curb and gutter to take care of too much rain. They don't own a tent. And even if they did, they have no hammer to pound in stakes and no hatchet to cut them.

What human beings have done to thwart the formidable powers of nature arrayed against them is really quite remarkable. Those who have led us, we've raised to hero status, from inventors like Copernicus to the buckskinned frontiersmen like Daniel Boone.

The moment humanity located shelter we turned on each other, and the misery that has resulted is unfathomable. Envy turned to anger, anger to theft, theft to murder, murder to war. Millions have perished.

But here again, we raise heroes, people who are somehow capable of looking at whatever problem looms up in front of them and scaling it by ingenuity or by sheer force of character and power of will. King David, George Washington, and Winston Churchill were leaders who brought their countries through war to peace.

But even in peace, the kingdom of God is always at odds with the kingdom of humankind. On one side, grace descends to bring the light of God into the hearts of the children of Adam and Eve. But Satan stands right at that point himself, Colossus-like, working diligently to bring to naught the cause of God Almighty.

Here too we have heroes—Noah, Abraham, Isaiah, Mary, the disciples and the apostles—all of them granted a spaciousness of soul. The children of God hold them in high esteem for the volume of their faith. Of course, Christ himself is the Supreme Leader, the Son of God and Son of man who vanquished death itself.

All our woes and miseries come from one of these sources—from nature, from our fellow people, or from the powers of Satan—and what all this adds up to is a battle. Don't let anyone tell you—sentimental believers or television commercials—that life is a breeze. It isn't. It's a battle, easier maybe for some than others. Many will face behemoth struggles that will demand heroism, whether it be against a drought that threatens the farm or cancer that threatens their lives; whether it be vicious rumors created in animosity or war itself; whether it be temptation in a thousand forms or even martyrdom.

Formidable walls arise against us throughout our lives, stand there monster-like, impregnable, unmovable. Injustice. We'll know it in our guts and see it in our own backyards, yet feel powerless in its grisly shadow. Sickness or death can prompt a despair so deep it becomes suicidal. Friends turn into enemies for reasons we don't understand. Our own sinful desires arise again and again despite our best efforts to hold them down.

Heroic courage is needed all through life, courage that comes from the strength of the Almighty. When the psalmist says, "By my God I leap over a wall," he does not mean to imply that his action is some out-of-body phenomenon. What he means to say is that with God in his heart, the greatest of inspirations the Holy Spirit can deliver, he knows that he can take on the width and breadth of any barrier or any wall before him.

What's miraculous is not so much the action as the strength to take it on, for we couldn't spring a lift off the ground without God's strength.

You know what's strange? Once they're up and over whatever wall presents itself before them, those heroes who know the real source of their strength will actually fall to their knees. And you know why.

EVER TOWARD
THE LORD

Mine eyes are ever toward the Lord.
—Psalm 25:15

No scriptural command is particularly easy to follow, but some seem humanly impossible: "pray without ceasing," for example. Not even time off to sleep? Who can possibly pray without ceasing? The Bible offers testimonies that are just as forbidding. The psalmist says, "I have set the LORD always before me" (16:8); and "Nevertheless, I am continually with thee" (73:23); and again, "Mine eyes are ever toward the LORD" (25:15).

The intent here is not "now and then." The lines say always, continually, without ceasing—in other words, *all the time*. Maybe this is simply poetic license, like the young and in love who gush poetically that they will love each other "till all the seas run dry."

Wrong. What Scripture testifies to is continual commitment, every day, every hour. It doesn't intend to infer that we can draw God to us, but instead that we allow God to draw us up, all the time, into the eternal. Our personal fellowship with God here in his world is the verifying prospect of what is perfectly heavenly in essence.

And that's not impossible, even though it seems terribly unlikely amid the zany and frantic lives we live. Neither David nor Paul were spiritual aesthetes, after all. Both knew our lives are more than endless devotional moments, and the world is no monastic cell.

Everyone has spiritual highs, times when, in some secluded spot, one's soul is not only alone with God but lost in him. We all seek those moments to escape from the world's busyness and to seek solitude that will fortify us for our return. But if that's all we know of spiritual life, then our lives are schizoid—one side without God and one with.

We don't exist to take vacations. People who require retreats for spiritual renewal often drug themselves against their own denial. When the retreats don't inspire, such people are inclined to give up, having missed the highs they so urgently need.

Uninterrupted, ceaseless continuation of fellowship with God doesn't depend on our thinking or planning, and it can't be willed. It must spring up from the inner motion of a heart in which the Holy Spirit has put down roots. If you know the Holy Spirit's indwelling, then you understand that intimacy with God happens whether or not we will it to happen. Like a mother tending her baby, the Holy Spirit is ever vigilant, even though the child sleeps.

What is at issue here is whether one's relationship, one's fellowship, grows in the heart and whether the inner disposition gradually attains a level of sanctification that opens us up to divine things. That's something that must occur.

Here's how it happens. For a time in our lives, we live outside of ourselves, not really understanding the nature of our hearts or our heart's commitments. Then awakenings occur, and we begin to know our strengths, our weaknesses, and what it is that goes on inside us. We discover God in the presence of the Holy Spirit, who takes compassion on us.

That knowledge carries us back into our lives with a firm sense of comfort and commitment. Our life outside—in business, profession, marriage, and family—begins to echo the music God creates in our souls. The two worlds mingle and permeate each other until we reach a point when our inner consciousness of God glows through everything we do, morning until night, with the Spirit's quickening strength.

This process begins with little more than holy mysticism, but it doesn't stop with our aroused feelings. The eye of the soul begins to discover more and more clearly that God dwells within us, but that he also can be known in our outside lives, where he shows himself equally omnipresent, ever drawing us to him.

Sin interrupts this process. There's no question about that. But as we come to see sin and feel it within us, the Spirit builds our resistance because we discover that the thought of losing God's presence—and the harmony he brings to our lives—would be disastrous.

The more deeply God comes to indwell, the more we see him in the busyness of our lives, and the more others see him in us. Then, our lives continually sing his praise.

THY VISITATION
HATH PRESERVED

Thou hast granted me life and favor,
and thy visitation hath preserved my spirit.
—Job 10:12

Although first impressions can sometimes be surprisingly accurate, they are never comprehensive. Perhaps a white shirt and tie say as much about who we are as do pierced body parts, but what's behind the physical image—that which we see immediately—is likely a great deal more than can be read in a tattoo, a diamond broach, or a black turtleneck.

We are *more* than our bodies.

"She gave up the ghost" is an old way of avoiding the word *death*, but its implication isn't inaccurate. When we die, something of us, our spirit, leaves our body behind like snake skin. All of us have this *spirit*, this breath of life. Although when we say someone "has spirit," we usually mean they've got get-up-and-go.

The two words *spirit* and *soul* are used very similarly, even in the Bible. When the psalmist cries out to the Lord, "thou hast delivered my soul from death" (116:8), he's referring, pure and simple, to his life. However, at times the word *soul* is used to mean one's spiritual existence. "My soul thirsteth for God, the living God" (Ps. 42:2) has little to do with a dry throat and everything to do with a parched soul.

Scripture doesn't distinguish between our life and our spirit. In God's Word our physical and spiritual existences are one. God formed humanity from the dust of the earth, but humanity came alive only when he breathed his breath into a set of lungs he'd already fashioned. *Soul* or *spirit* doesn't have much existence without a self, a person.

This soul or spirit isn't disposable. We can make it dirty, but we can't take it off like a dirty sweatshirt. Our souls live on long after we've shucked our physical selves.

Whatever it is, however it looks, and wherever it abides in our bodies, we know this—God keeps an eye on all of our souls. This is Job's confession: "Thou hast granted me life and favor, and thy visitation hath preserved my spirit." God *visits* our spirits, and not simply as if he were observing teatime. That's not the meaning here. God's *always* there, watching, guiding, directing. He's in charge. He's supervising.

It takes some time before we really come to understand his presence watching over us. Often that recognition comes initially in extraordinary circumstance—grief, fear, sadness. Maybe we're afraid of being hurt or killed. A huge storm threatens the family. For the first time, on our knees, we come passionately to the Supervisor.

But as we mature, we come to understand his attention is broader and wider. For instance, we scream at our kids and guilt oppresses us. Why? Because the Supervisor places our conscience up against our anger to show us how we didn't measure up. Part of supervision is evaluation. The supervisor watches us, lets us know when we're not getting the work done right.

But conscience and guilt are still only a part of the Supervisor's work because he also protects us, keeps the lines going, and keeps us supplied. Once again, the more we come to hear his voice, the more we begin to understand how pervasive his voice is in our lives—not simply to condemn or criticize, but to usher in joy, to reward us, to bring us our checks. The more we know of his presence, the greater he appears.

His supervision is so comprehensive that it began already with bygone ancestors, long before our birth. It continues through our childhood, our lives as adults, and into our retirement years. Throughout our lives, we plan careers, job transfers, retirement funds, and family reunions; some of us even plan our own funerals. But when we're gone, our supervision of our own lives ends. Not his. Not even when we die does the Supervisor of our souls leave us for another job. His plan for us is much more wide-ranging because it stretches on forever into eternity.

One can, without too much problem, seriously grieve the Holy Spirit in rejecting God's supervision of our souls and spirits; or one can choose to work with him. There is that much freedom. But whatever we choose, he's there, watching and waiting.

EVERY ONE WHICH
SEETH THE SON

He that hath seen me hath seen the Father;
and how sayest thou then, [Philip,] Show us the Father?
—John 14:9

At the heart of every word we've been saying and thinking is a very, very simple idea. Everyone who has ever heard the gospel knows the words. Children believe it. Old folks testify to the comfort of its reality.

This is it—the whole truth and nothing but the truth, so help us God: *Nothing under the sun or above it, on this earth or beneath it, is as meaningful or consequential as Jesus Christ, God's Son and our Lord and Savior.* Bottom line. End of story.

Our most significant task in all of life, according to Jesus Christ himself, is to believe in him: "This is the work of God, that ye believe on him whom he has sent" (John 6:29). Why? The gospel of John answers that question straightforwardly: "And he that believeth not the Son shall not see life; but the wrath of God abideth on him" (3:36).

We're not talking about a superficial religiousness here, nor the deepest of personal, pious inclinations. What is commanded is not simply a willed acceptance of the validity of deity, a kind of shoulder-shrugging, "Well, of course I believe." Faith in Jesus Christ, his presence or absence in your heart, is the ultimate litmus test. To believe in him is the most consequential act we humans face.

The word is *saved.* Don't miss it. To know, truly and sincerely, the all-embracing, all-permeating, complete and perfect happiness of Christ is what all of this is about, even though the source of our faith—how we come to it—itself remains, and will remain, a mystery.

For centuries the church has tried to define faith. Sometimes it has done that too intellectually, creating a cold head knowledge with no spiritual glow. Sometimes the church entertains its mystery in the human heart with too much enthusiasm and thereby creates cheap mysticism that evaporates once the fervid heat has left the affections.

Nothing is more important than faith in Christ. Nothing can be placed beside it, nothing substituted. Either faith in him brings deliverance, or there is no deliverance, for us individually and for the world. Faith is a gift, but it requires our assent. It is a divine seed we must nurture. It affects our emotions powerfully, but it also makes intellectual demands. There are some things we simply have to know: Who is Christ? What did he do? What did he mean? Where is he now? What is our future? These questions need answers, and those answers need to be learned, inside and out.

But knowledge of Jesus' life is not the same as seeing Jesus. Again, the gospel of John says, "every one which seeth the Son, and believeth on him, may have everlasting life" (6:40). Seeing Jesus is not simply a moving experience or an intellectual grasp of his character. Seeing Jesus demands all of our affections, our intelligence, and our will. Everything we know and feel about the Savior must be reduced to the unity of the image of the Son of God. Every inner impulse and sensation, every holy emotion, must merge into this image if we are to enjoy it fully. And its grasp must never let up, must keep us engaged, transport us through life with Christ—who is God in us.

It may be hard to believe, but we have it better than the disciples. While they saw him face to face, few of them understood how wholly of God he really was. We know. Therefore, we know him better. The ascension hasn't impoverished us in the least. We're enriched by his being with the Father because, in him, we are enriched too. Knowing Christ means knowing the Father. It means eternity.

Nothing—anywhere, anytime, anyplace—matters more than Jesus Christ. Why? Listen to the petition in the high priestly prayer: "[Holy Father, I pray thee,] that they all may be one; as thou, Father, art in me, and I in thee, that they also may be one in us: that the world may believe that thou hast sent me" (John 17:21). That's what it's all about.

In an Even Place

My foot standeth in an even place.
—Psalm 26:12

A life without care, anxiety, sorrow, and disappointment—if such a life exists—is probably too sweet for our own good. Like rich chocolate, a life of ease goes down smoothly but clogs our veins. When we have it too easy, we start to believe one of two things, both equally erroneous: that we've done it all ourselves, pulled ourselves up by our own bootstraps; or that God has blessed us because, well, we're good people.

Prosperity elevates ego. Ease enervates. When income inflates, so does our self-concept. While others stumble, we start to think we are truly blessed with vision. We gain an opinion of our excellence that nurses sinful pride and simultaneously chokes the compassion required to love those not so nobly blessed.

People with a bulging sense of their own goodness tend to deflate dramatically at the onset of trouble. Everything collapses, built as it is on faith in self. There's no disciplined strength, nothing to hold them up in the struggle against hurt and grief. Often, perplexity occurs—"How can this happen? Why me?"—and then despair. The high and mighty, brought low, suddenly lack the courage to live and hope for the future.

If one's life has been traveled along a straight and flat freeway, then the verse in question today—"My foot standeth in an even path"—may sound like simple self-confidence. But it's much more.

Consider those who struggle—against poverty, injustice, bigotry, or outright hatred. Many do. Consider those who live their entire lives struggling with ill health. Consider those constantly fearing for kids who have gone wrong and who show no desire to return. Consider those who lose their children to untimely death. Some of us have struggled with disappointment for an entire lifetime. Such sadness can end in despair.

But we all know others whose faith, with God's help, has pulled them back up, people who have not given up hope and who can say with Habakkuk: "Although the fig tree shall not blossom, neither shall fruit be in the vines; . . . and there shall be no herd in the stalls: Yet I will rejoice in the Lord" (3:17-18).

Think of Lazarus. The man spent his entire lifetime in the service of rich fools, sweeping up the crumbs from their table. If he saw his daughter graduate from medical school, we don't know of it. Jesus tells us nothing else of the man's life. And yet, there he is in glory, while the rich folks arrayed in all their finery tragically party on down below.

Some people, grievously afflicted with cancer or some other horrible disease, pray unceasingly and still fall off into the grave. We all know those people.

The fact is, none of us has a *right* to anything. Those who have suffered know only too well that we will never stand before the face of God and demand anything—not happiness, not even deliverance from misery. Listen to the words of Jesus: "O my Father, if it be possible, let this cup pass from me: nevertheless not as I will, but as thou wilt" (Matt. 26:39).

The real miracle is those who can say that their feet are planted firmly on the ground *in the very horror of their adversity.* That's the most glorious way to read this verse. When nothing is before us but a craggy mountainous path fraught with danger, when the cross of suffering casts its shadow over us even into the grave, then only the full glory of faith stubbornly discloses to us a higher way, a way to the top of the mountain of God's holiness, a way that dissolves all sorrow and misery and agony in a much, much higher vision of reality.

In pleasure or distress, in grief and gladness, in prosperity and adversity, the person whose soul remains confident and whose heart is undaunted, that person lifts the most joyful testimony of all when she says, "It is well with my soul."

A WEALTHY PLACE

Thou hast caused men to ride over our heads;
we went through fire and through water:
but thou broughtest us out into a wealthy place.
—Psalm 66:12

Someday there will be no more redemption—who'll need it? Someday there will be no more miraculous healing—no one will be sick. Someday there will be no more need for comfort—all our distress will end. Every difficulty that interrupts our joy and disturbs our lives will be forever vanquished. There will be no need for us to renew our strength or have our faith refreshed. That's heaven, and to our earthly eyes it seems not at all a familiar place.

Which is not to say that the hereafter will be an eternal bore. Even though we know a whole lot less about life after death than people like to think we know, what is certain is that our new understanding of God will be richer than anything we even dreamed of in our finest musical tributes, our most blessed sermons, or our deepest meditations. The blind will see—and that includes all of us. On earth, we all walk with white canes.

Sin's influence is profound and constant in our lives. That doesn't mean our entire lives are laid waste by sin's heavy artillery, nor does it suggest we violate God's law every last second of every last minute. But we know this: sin brings breakup, temporarily removes the supports of our faith, and twists the paths of our lives. We all suffer ups and downs, pleasure and pain, health and sickness, joy and sorrow. We all get tired, then regain strength to go on.

If sin is singularly responsible for all of our misery—for our most awful headaches, for cancer and AIDS and rebellious kids, for depression and lower back pain, for unemployment, alcoholism, and homelessness—then it is, in part, responsible also for our healing methods—for medicine and polio vaccines, for judges and justice, for politics and recovery programs, social workers and ministers of the gospel. There will be no steeples in glory, after all, because our society will need no separate place of worship.

Our trials and tribulations can sometimes last months and even years; but in God's plan they finally give way to the refreshment of our Spirit, which—after the deprivation—comes into our lives in a vivid celebration of joy. The thrill of victory is never sweeter than when sin lies defeated behind us.

No one knew this better than the psalmist, who often, in back-to-back psalms, stumbles into valleys abysmally low, then climbs with seeming effortlessness to Himalayan heights. Sometimes the psalmist remembers radical change in a single verse, as here: "Thou hast caused men to ride over our heads; we went through fire and through water: but thou broughtest us out into a wealthy place" (66:12).

Some of us, seemingly, suffer much more than others. Only through God's grace and a measure of heroic human character can some of us make it through the fray. Yet, we all know heavily burdened people who find life much more abundant than those who walk almost effortlessly over little more than rolling hills.

Wealth, in the psalmist's song, is something more than diamonds or gold, more than the baubles at the end of human rainbows. *Wealth*, in this verse, suggests the end of deprivation, the surcease of troubles. God's deliverance from those who crack heads is, for the believer, a *wealthy place*, as the psalmist says.

What it means really is a return to being close to God; we return to the wealth of God's presence after his seemingly long, long absence. Only those who know God personally and deeply, who have come near unto him, can know the pain and sorrow in his being gone. And when he returns, or we do, only such believers can appreciate the profuse blessings of being refreshed once more with his presence.

Only then can we see that God was operating upon us in grace, even in our sorrow. At that point, one comes to understand that without poverty there would be no wealth in Christ; without valleys there would be no mountains; without suffering, no joy. Only then can we know his presence as our comfort in every situation.

FROM STRENGTH
TO STRENGTH

*They go from strength to strength, every one of
them in Zion appeareth before God.*
—Psalm 84:7

When an oak tree stands only five feet high, you can bend the young trunk in your hand. When a colt is born, its first stumble-bum jaunt across the corral seems vaudevillian. A baby, totally dependent upon its mother, first learns to creep, then walk, and then run away.

Physical growth is in evidence all around us; but we also grow in other ways, none so cleanly documented as, say, changes in shoe size. Soon enough, children begin to confront life on their own. Artists grow in their ability to communicate their vision. Training, education, and life experience broadens their understanding and sharpens their abilities with colors or words or music.

Most all of us grow in willpower. We can become better teachers, better mothers, better doctors. Ballplayers learn to be better hitters by watching a wide variety of pitches and pitchers. We move, in life, from strength to strength.

But the examples we've considered do not fully explain what the psalmist means, because the examples do not include the life of divine grace. Here, too, we must grow and develop, or else we will lose ground. As we know, nothing really stands still. Things either improve or slip into decline.

And, progress does have an end, after all. A mule will never grow into a thoroughbred. What's more, in every living thing the process of growth is stymied by age. The artist loses a wrist to arthritis. A horse's legs go eventually, just like a ballplayer's. The sharpness of the most brilliant of philosophers eventually grows dull.

What's amazing is this—only in our moral lives can we continue to grow. Love and devotion can increase in us to the very brink of the grave. Our arms may give out, but our characters can be made Samson-like.

But simply by growing old, we don't grow stronger in character. We really should be able to see distinct growth in character, don't you think? When, years later, you run into someone you knew as a kid, you should be able to see that she grew in character, grew in love and commitment.

But is such growth always visible? Can we say that, at forty, we are (or were) twice as dependent upon the Lord as we were at twenty? Think of the chinks in your own personality. Are they still with you decades after you discovered them? For most of us, the answer is yes. When you were a kid, some friend of yours had this annoying habit of wanting to upstage everybody—always having to have the last word. After twenty years you meet that person once again, and what does he do but go on and on in the exact same way he did a quarter century before.

But why talk about others? Do you still too regularly stick your foot in your mouth? Do you still hide from trouble whenever you can? Do you still fail to assert yourself and then leave conversations seething because you didn't say what was on your mind? Some things, it seems, don't change.

One can become converted to God, set his or her mind on holy things, and in all sorts of ways turn over a new leaf. We can be confident that the old man of sin is exiled to some dusty closet. We think of ourselves as new creations, brand-new people. But still that old man emerges for more than a few celebrated appearances.

For most of us a certain level of faith becomes more or less fixed. We don't grow. We begin to feed on what happened to us earlier in our lives and start to tell old stories almost exclusively. We might grow a little smarter, gain in experience and even in spiritual wisdom, but we don't come to a higher strength in our walk with God.

Sometimes old folks, just like kids, backslide, strive after nothing higher, and become satisfied with who they are. And that's where they stay.

Not everyone, however. Some saints act like giant floodlights, showering everyone around them with grace. Some older folks never cease taking full draughts of God's love from the cup of grace. Some grow from strength to strength.

Wouldn't it be wonderful if we all grew continually in the faith? Try to guess what life might be like in your family, in your church, even in society, if all of us moved so constantly, so unceasingly, from strength to strength. Just imagine.

BLESSED ARE THE PURE IN HEART

Blessed are the pure in heart: for they shall see God.
—Matthew 5:8

An impossible goal stands imploringly before every sincere Christian: we want to be sinless, but we know we never will be. Even in Psalm 51, King David's sorrow for sin was not enough to purify his heart. "Create in me a clean heart, O God," he begged (v. 10), but not until death could he ever offer an unsullied heart to God Almighty. Like all of us, King David wanted intensely to have a purity of heart he could never have, totally.

Christians are not the only members of society who desire purity of heart. Unbelievers still esteem those individuals they consider "pure," but their definitions differ. To an unbelieving mind, purity of heart means high moral character. To the Christian, it means something more.

What we have said here needs to be explained in deep humility and not without fear and trembling. In this life, knowing who is and who is not a child of God is very, very difficult. Some of the Lord's own barely dare to admit this to themselves. Some are his, but show it very little. On the other hand, some chatter on and on so much about their being his that one wonders whether they aren't deceiving themselves.

It's embarrassing to admit, but too often in life, unbelievers don't look a bit different than believers, at least not in moral character. Look at King David's blunders, or listen to Paul: "For the good that I would I do not" (Rom. 7:19). We're not talking about hypocrites here either—that's another category altogether. We're talking here about people who consider themselves God's own family, who want to live righteously. They're sometimes tough to spot.

No one is without sin. Believers know that. Therefore, the children of God fight the sin in their own hearts as if it were mortal combat—because it is. They know deeply that evil darkens the entire span of their lives. Fighting that sin is arduous work.

When Christ laid out the Beatitudes, he was describing a single state of mind and heart, not necessarily a variety of believers. All of the descriptions—to be meek, to be peacemakers, to mourn—are meant to describe the same kind of persons: those who place themselves under the guardianship of Jesus and want to enter his kingdom. To be pure in heart should not be misunderstood to mean sinless. If Jesus meant this beatitude only for those who had never entertained a miserable thought or done a regrettable sin, we should all despair. To the moment of death, we all fight iniquity.

This is not to say that the Christian does not make progress toward righteousness. The more we grow in faith, the more keen our eye becomes in understanding faith and fleeing evil. Even though the world is befuddled by a truly saintly person who pleads passionately to be free from sin, those who know their sinful condition inside and out, know only too well that sin often lurks even in their most virtuous acts.

In some ways, we might consider that we have two selves—one of which is, by the nature of our fallen humanity, sullied by sin; but another self which is capable of understanding that condition and arming itself against giving in to its baseness.

We cannot be pure as long as we live on earth, but we can grow towards purity in our attitude toward the poisonous inclinations of the heart. When we begin to hate the evil that is within us, when we struggle against our mortal natures, battle against sin with every ounce of strength the Lord gives, then we say with Christ, "Deliver us from evil."

We can be pure in our attempts to fight the impurity that wells up from our own hearts. Believers who lose the conscientious desire to flee evil all too easily sink away in the murky waters of the sinful condition all of us share.

But if, with God's help, we struggle against our own darkness, we can be pure in our attempts to fight it, even though our hearts will never be without sin. With God as ally, Satan cannot bully us. This struggle will bring us ever closer and closer to God, and in that position—and that position only—will we see God with the eye of a soul dedicated to him.

Thou Holdest Mine Eyes Waking

Thou holdest mine eyes waking:
I am so troubled that I cannot speak.
—Psalm 77:4

Generally, people close their eyes in prayer, just as they do in sleep. Although the differences between sleep and prayer are obvious, sometimes they are more alike than one might think.

Just as we shut our eyes in sleep, we also shut them in prayer to avoid distraction. But in prayer we want to focus our attention on what we're doing—talking to God. Christ himself suggested this posture when he said that people should go into their closets and shut the door behind them when they pray. Furthermore, often as not in his ministry, Jesus withdrew from the crowds that followed him in order to pray in the wilderness or the mountains, where there was less distraction. Even at Gethsemane he looked for a lonely spot for his last petitions to his Father.

On rare occasions, people may fall asleep in public prayer. More often, however, our minds simply wander. The distractions we seek to avoid make us their victims by way of our own active imaginations. Soon enough, we're far removed, our thoughts scurrying around the globe, while someone in front or beside us is actually praying.

Prayer and sleeping are radically different in consciousness. In sleep, we seek to deaden our sense of what's going on; in prayer, we seek to quicken it. When we pray, what we want more than anything—at least in private—is to shut out all other considerations in order to focus intently and intensely on talking with God. We want a higher consciousness, not a lower one—certainly not the near unconsciousness we all want when we hit the pillow.

Even though we want unconsciousness in sleep, many of us never reach it. Dreams plague some of us. While we still don't understand a great deal about the nature of our dreams, we do know that dreams are sometimes prophecy, creating odd little particles of memory that suddenly occur in our conscious hours—what is called déjà vu. Sometimes dreams put us into shivers it takes us hours to come out of. Sometimes we'd rather not think about what we saw or felt in our dreams. But what's clear to those of us who are great dreamers is that our dreams—for good or ill—can and do keep us awake.

But sleep—or lack of it—prompts another kind of consciousness in many of us, a condition best described, simply, as sleeplessness. Sadly enough, some of us toss and turn, scrunch the pillow, count sheep, and pull all kinds of stunts in an attempt to fall into that deadened state we desire so much after hard and active days. Many causes exist for sleeplessness: sickness, nervous agitation, and guilt are just a few.

Asaph's distress makes him sleepless, but he admits that God's own fingers kept his eyes from closing: "I cried out to God with my voice . . . and he gave ear unto me. In the day of my trouble I sought the Lord: my sore ran in the night, and ceased not: my soul refused to be comforted. I remembered God, and was troubled: I complained, and my spirit was overwhelmed. Thou holdest mine eyes waking: I am so troubled that I cannot speak" (Ps. 77:1-4). Yet, when we read the entire psalm, Asaph's woe becomes the occasion for his testimony to God's faithfulness.

For those of us whose lights don't go out the moment we stretch our bodies on a bed, it might be useful to think of Psalm 77 and consider that we can use our waking moments—even when we'd rather be asleep—to commune with God. Sleepless hours can be a gold mine. Many believers have been spiritually enriched by using their own sleeplessness.

It's remarkable—it's miraculous really—that a God who loves us can use even the occasion of our distress, our sleeplessness, to create opportunity for a closer and more intimate walk with him. The work of God on the souls of his people goes on even in the wee hours of a sleepless night, bringing glory to his name.

I WAIT FOR THEE
ALL THE DAY LONG

*Lead me in thy truth, and teach me: for thou art
the God of my salvation; on thee do I wait all the day.*
—Psalm 25:5

Every believer keeps a picture of the apostles stored away in memory, a gathering of robed saints, their long-haired heads adorned with dancing tongues of fire. That picture is no still life—it's a film clip, complete with sound. What might be mistaken for babbling is going on almost riotously. But it's not gibberish, because those robed folks actually understand what they're saying to each other. It's Pentecost, and it's an incredible picnic.

The rich grace of Pentecost, the outpouring of the Holy Spirit, is an event known and loved by the church alone, the high and holy privilege of the ransomed of the Lord. No unbelievers attend that picnic.

But the Holy Spirit does not belong to believers alone. Nothing in this wide world exists or operates without the visitation of the Spirit of God. The Almighty invests his Spirit into gravity, into the motion of the surf, into bats and birds and bananas. The Holy Spirit is all around us, and the church itself risks silly mysticism or hyper-spirituality when we begin to think that we alone are recipients of the Spirit's power.

What does belong to the church alone, however, is the special knowledge of Pentecost. A star in the universe understands nothing of the Spirit's power. A plant is largely devoid of sense. But nothing under heaven, no animal or any living thing, connects itself with the holiness of God like humanity does, and none as deeply and thankfully as the church, the body of believers.

What phenomenal assurance it is to know that this Spirit—his Spirit—will never leave the church, the body of Christ, the mystical body of which he is the head. In this body, the Holy Ghost dwells, first in the head and then in all its members.

It goes without saying that not every single member of the visible church *knows* God. Many can know God in the way a close reading of the New Testament can acquaint us with Paul of Tarsus. But knowing Paul through his words is not the same as knowing him personally, face-to-face. And so it is with God. Not everyone who reads his Word really *knows* him, intimately and fully. Not everyone who lives a moral life comes near unto him through the operation of the Spirit.

However, the true church of God, whose members are not written up in any membership book here on earth, is within the visible church—those who practice the Christian faith. So while the two aren't identical, they share many members. Here's our joy: the church we can see on city streets—like the invisible church—lives only by the Holy Spirit, whose constant attention keeps it alive *because* the church we see contains the invisible church. And that's why the faithful, visible church provides, through preaching and the sacraments, the only real taste of fellowship with the Eternal Being. That kind of experience does not exist outside of the congregation of believers.

But *fellowship* is not simply coffee and cookies or good conversation. Fellowship with God occurs individually in the existential meeting of self with the Almighty, ego to ego, in the mysticism of grace. The fellowship of the Spirit allows us to meet God in person, to know him—not occasionally as we know our friends, but constantly as we know our parents. A child assumes a parent's constant concern, relies on the immutability of a parental presence. Even in adulthood, children know their parents' ubiquitous concern.

And so it is with the believer who knows God's abiding presence. Distractions come in the way and our impure hearts rupture the union. At times God himself creates a distance. But true believers have no rest until their communion with God is reestablished, day-in, day-out.

For the true child of God, only two conditions are possible: either we are in fellowship, or we wait for that intimacy. "On thee do I wait," says the psalmist, "all the day."

O GOD, MY GOD!

Then will I go unto the altar of God, unto God my exceeding
joy: yea, upon the harp will I praise thee, O God my God.
—Psalm 43:4

I t's probably in poor taste to sing out "O God, my God!" too frequently. Anyone who does so certainly risks appearing pretentious or
self-important or, at least, seems to show a covetous kind of selfishness.
When believers go on and on about *my* God, it's easy for others to believe
they could care less for anyone else. Christ's own model prayer does not
begin with the individual, even though it uses personal pronouns. "*Our*
Father" is much better, isn't it? "Give *us* this day *our* daily bread." We don't
stand before God alone, but in the fellowship of love with all God's saints.

Nonetheless, the psalmist's resounding testimony, "O God, my God!"
is the avowal of the believer who knows his Father's eternal love. And
when we can say those words because we know that love, it is the soul's
booming affirmation of being known intimately by the Creator.

But that mature knowledge is something we grow to and into.
Consider a child, who learns to pray by mimicking Mom and Dad. For
years that child's prayer, no matter how deeply meant and felt, is limited
by the range of his understanding and experience. We can be tickled by
kids' prayers, but they are kiddish, childish.

Sometime along the line, the child begins to take the practice of
prayer—the folded hands, the closed eyes, the silence—and appropriate it
for himself. At some moment in their lives, all believing kids pray on their
own. When they do, they know prayer and fellowship in a way that they
never had experienced before. For many kids, this begins to happen some-

where around the age of ten or twelve, when the world starts to look a bit bigger and more formidable than it did from their limited and egocentric childish perspectives. Prayer becomes more than custom or quaint behavior. It becomes real.

But from a parent's standpoint, that's a risky time in the life of a child. The protective idealism of childhood—even the idealism of prayer and faith—gets tested by what children begin to see as a more and more hazardous world facing them. The difference between appearance and reality suddenly stands front and center. For some kids, the radical difference between the dark world and the joy of childish faith makes them abandon prayer as silly idealism, as an infantile escape from the real world. For others, more fearful, the idealism of faith is so attractive that they hide in piety and practice a sickly mysticism that can easily master the soul.

But in the ordinary pilgrimage to mature faith, spiritual stability emerges from that period of struggle. The mature Christian begins more and more to understand the relation between the life of the soul and life in the world. Heroic devotion to one's task in life goes hand in hand with a life of prayer that develops ever more richly. Our work and our prayer becomes almost one as prayer becomes more instantaneous and regular, less patterned by obligation or public necessity. We begin to understand the command to pray without ceasing. We begin to understand that we live in God's presence every minute of the day.

But amazingly, our personal pilgrimages are all different. It's thrilling to understand that God knows that, that he cares for us individually, that he watches our steps on our own individual pilgrimages, that he cares for us all along our separate paths—and that he has done so from before time itself. His love and care are constant. What makes us different is us—not him. And yet he cares; yet he watches; yet he loves.

It is a testimony to God's glory that he gives each of us his fellowship even in our differences and that he allows us to grow at our own rate and in our own time. Each of us approach his throne in a unique and personal way that encompasses every aspect of our individuality, expressing our separate experiences, our predilections, and our personalities. He knows us intimately as individuals, yet he loves us as his children.

That's what allows us to say, with the psalmist, "Oh God, *my* God!" ▧

THE LORD IS
THY SHADE

*The LORD is thy keeper: the LORD is
thy shade upon thy right hand.
—Psalm 121:5*

T he old line that "a picture is worth a thousand words" may help us
understand the whole world's fascination with movies. Even
though book sales don't appear to be falling, cinema arrests the attention
of hundreds of millions of people on a weekly basis. There's something in
us, it seems, that would rather see than read, perhaps because seeing is
easier than doing the thinking required by reading.

But knowing by seeing is not as bad as some writers and literature
teachers might want us to believe. Nowhere does the Bible say that only
systematic theologians or devoted readers will enjoy the hereafter. What
quality or characteristic will link all of those blessed with eternal life—red
and yellow, black and white, old and young, smart and simple—is the deep
desire to *see* God, to know him fully.

"Lord, show us the Father," says Philip, expressing clearly this longing.
The apostles gloried in the fact that they had actually seen Jesus (John
21:25), and yet they also said that now we see only darkly, but someday we
shall see face to face (1 Cor. 13:13). Notice that there's nothing in those
verses about reading theology. What they speak of is the experience of
Christ—seeing him. As John says in his first letter, "Beloved . . . it does not
yet appear what we shall be: but we know that, when he shall appear, we
shall be like him; for we shall see him as he is" (3:2).

Ancient Bibles were filled with illustrations, even though they included
no pictures. Visual imagery has always helped us to see the intent of God's

Word. When Jesus Christ describes himself as the vine, the shepherd, or the lamb, he uses pictures we know from the world around us, images borrowed from nature and life in order to bring the spiritual closer to us.

God is a rock, a high tower, a shield, a keeper, Father, and King. He sits on his throne. And here's another, a gem: "The Lord is thy shade upon thy right hand" (Ps. 121:5). Isaiah uses the same idea: "For thou hast been a strength to the poor, a strength to the needy in his distress, a refuge from the storm, *a shadow from the heat*" (25:4).

In some coastal regions especially it's hard to imagine that anyone might want shelter from the sun. Some of us see it so infrequently, we celebrate its appearance. But in the desert the sun is an oppressor. People wear white to avoid it and build thick walls to insulate themselves from its heavy hand. Where the temperature hovers at the unbearable for weeks and months, every living thing seeks the shade.

Against what? Against the sun. None of us—not even the boldest, the most powerful, the smartest—can take the constant heat, figuratively or literally. Stress—and distress—comes into our lives, as all of us know, in many forms. What is assumed here is a force that is constant in its advance, a swarm of trouble that's wilting in its pressure. Like desert heat, it parches our throat and makes us speechless. In the methodical assault of that kind of debilitating force, God is our shade. This is not a macho image and has no flexed biceps. Shade is our relief. When the only posture is prostration, God offers us shelter.

The medium is a cloud, which removes us from the heat. A father can, by his own size, become a shadow for his child on a walk through the desert sun. This is the picture the psalmist brings to mind in "thy shade upon thy right hand"—a father, taking the heat.

Here is our comfort: God does not, and mercifully will not, leave us alone. And the fact is, everyone walks in a desert. Nobody was ever promised a rose garden. But the Lord follows us through the heat, hovers over us, cloud-like, bringing us shelter, enabling us to go on and even pick up the pace.

We know this kind of biblical poetry well. It's no fiction. That God is our shade is the honest-to-God truth. When the assault of the sun threatens to wilt us to parched tomato vines, his shadow comes over us and stands at our right hand, stands near unto us, taking the heat.

HE INCLINED HIS
EAR UNTO ME

Because he hath inclined his ear unto me, therefore will I call
upon him as long as I live.
—Psalm 116:2

Presidents and prime ministers surround themselves with only their most devoted friends, men and women whose opinions they trust and whose personal allegiance they know with certainty. If one isn't part of that select circle, the only access to real political clout is by way of that circle of trusted confidantes. Not everyone gets an ear. The access to power in politics is strictly controlled.

At least one of the definitions of politics is "the use of strategy or intrigue in obtaining power or status." But anyone with a dime's worth of street sense knows that politics, as in "playing politics," is not an activity limited to the world of government and law. Relationships between husband and wife, between parent and child, between teacher and student, between labor and management—in fact, all relationships—require some politics, some use of strategy or intrigue in obtaining power or status.

All relationships except one. The King of kings has no purebred court of special friends. He doesn't surround himself with minions to winnow out the requests of those folks for whom he doesn't have time. Before God, Mother Theresa's prayer is no more vital than a mass murderer's, if that prayer is truly meant. God's kingdom is the only true democracy.

He inclines his ear to us, no matter what our station, no matter whether the prayer is being shouted before a Million Man March or stammered in the tattered remains of a mobile home just destroyed by a tornado. He listens to governors, bishops, chairpersons, blue bloods; but he won't turn away from the street waifs, the homeless, the abused, or the powerless. Station, rank, pedigree, diploma, all mean nothing. He inclines his ear to everyone he loves.

It is a mark of grace to know that God listens, that he actually bends over to hear our prayers. There are, of course, millions of people praying; and there are, additionally, dozens of kinds of prayers, spoken and unspoken—prayers done from custom and done spontaneously; prayers created by necessity, by deep care, fear, or grief; and prayers uttered out of joy, praise, or sheer exultation. Some are public, more are private; some are offered in sweat and tears, others in emotional ecstasy. That he hears them all, that he inclines his ear at all to any of us, is proof of his grace.

Sometimes, like the psalmist, we plead without words. We don't regularly call those utterances prayers. What we call *prayers* are the words that come through our consciousness. We know what we want to pray for, and those ideas are expressed in words and phrases we formulate. These words we bring before the Father, who his Son directed us to address "in heaven."

But to address God in that way is to admit that an entire universe stands between us and the King of kings. It's interesting that Christ doesn't suggest we begin by addressing the Holy Spirit within us, but instead starts as if our Father were removed from us eternally. The Heidelberg Catechism says such an address in itself reminds us that our concerns should not be "earthly."

But what begins at a distance slowly but surely shrinks into intimacy. God comes closer as we ask. He enters our hearts as the Holy Spirit prays with us and for us, even prompts us to address the Almighty. Prayers that begin as if the Spirit in us were speaking are mystic nonsense. We begin at a distance and, in the process of prayer, draw ever nearer as we "lift up our hearts unto the Lord" and he inclines his ear to us.

Then, when the distance shrinks, the praying soul finds rest, and the pray-er turns truly to God. We become, in true prayer, on-line with the King of kings.

In that way, prayer itself is the seal of his everlasting love. Prayer is both process and end because it brings us to God *and* signifies our closeness. Those who know God face-to-face understand that even if our prayers are not immediately answered, our intimacy with the undisputed ruler of all nations and all time makes us more confident that we are—and forever will be—his own children.

TAKE NOT THY HOLY SPIRIT FROM ME

And take not thy Holy Spirit from me.
—Psalm 51:11

After King David recognizes his most horrendous sins, he brings this request before the Lord: "Take not thy holy spirit from me." That petition seems somewhat presumptuous, doesn't it? After his adultery and murder, we're likely to wonder whether the Spirit is anywhere in the vicinity of his heart and soul. How arrogant to assume the Spirit hasn't long ago abandoned him. The man has walked away from God and stepped beyond the Spirit's favor.

Just exactly how God operates in our lives is a mysterious miracle, but still very much worth our own befuddled attempts to understand. To sense the nature of David's pleading here requires some searching on our part.

What happens in us as we mature as Christians occurs in three steps. First, we begin to seek his face. To do that we have to turn our back on the world's vanities and begin to open our eyes to the more brilliant light of his countenance. That's step one.

Then, once we focus more surely on the Lord, the light of his face begins to light our own. We start to reflect the brilliance of his love for us. We become more than receivers. We become mirrors of his divine compassion.

Finally—and now we come to the most mysterious step—God sends his Spirit to make our hearts his home. We become, in a more intimate sense than ever before, one with the Lord. Our fellowship becomes a person-to-person, face-to-face conversation. This step, as impossible as it is to describe with words, is the highest reality of the Christian life, and it only occurs after some time.

But this close communion can be lost. Our own human shoddiness, our sin, the pressures of temptations and desires can and do interrupt our intimate fellowship with God through his Spirit, because that relationship is extremely delicate. When anything comes between us and the Holy Spirit within us, communication breaks down. It's extremely difficult for us to hold up our end of that relationship because our end is as weak as our humanity. Like David, we fall. Our grasp is so tenuous that a wince of hesitation injures the Spirit's touch in our lives. That's the way it is here below.

But here's the glory. Even when we drop the ball, the Holy Spirit does not depart. He stays with us. This is mysterious and very much beyond description. Still we can understand some things about the Spirit's operations from utterances like David's. What we must come to see is the overwhelming power of God's love—that even in our most treacherous iniquity, the Spirit will not quit on us. He may recede. He may well lock the gates to the tabernacle he inhabits within us. But he will not depart. Such is God's amazing, divine love for us, his imagebearers, his children. He won't quit, even when we do.

From our vantage point, the Spirit may appear gone. We know we don't deserve his favor. We know our sin and may think it presumptuous to assume he is still with us. But we're dead wrong. Even in our moments of deepest rebellion, we still retain this sense of knowing where we belong. That direction-making is the Spirit's prompting.

On his knees, David comes to God in his sin, because even in the monstrous groaning of his guilt, even in the desolation of his banishment, the Holy Spirit still guides him back to something he knows he's loathingly rejected. So too with us. We may feel ourselves forever lost, but our souls, in touch with God through the indwelling of his Spirit, come to know this peace—that grace does not and will not let go. It's still working. Then the one anxious fear we still have is David's: "Take not thy Holy Spirit from me."

When that prayer is answered, the soul's tabernacle will be reopened and the joy of salvation will be experienced again. Blessed is that person who, even in sin, comes to experience that kind of return to the Spirit's favor. Those who know that desolation, know also and intimately the comfort the Spirit brings to those who are near to God.

KNOW YE NOT THAT
YE ARE THE TEMPLE
OF GOD

Know ye not that ye are the temple of God,
and that the Spirit of God dwelleth in you?
—1 Corinthians 3:16

Humanity has a fondness for gathering cultural characteristics into certain eras. We speak of the Roaring Twenties, the Fifties, and the Sixties, as well as the Age of Enlightenment, the Romantic Age, and the Post-Modern Era. Yet we don't talk all that much about a historic date when everything changed, the day of Pentecost. What started that day began an era so radically different from that which came before that we could well revise our calendars. When the Holy Spirit came into the hearts of believers, the separation between God and humanity fell away into oblivion.

Before Pentecost, God lived at a certain place—on Mt. Zion, for instance. If you wanted to visit, you knew where to travel because the Creator had an address, a neighborhood. But after Pentecost, he made our hearts his home. He sent his Holy Spirit not only *to* us, but *into* us.

And everything changed. Unbelievers no longer see the temple of God. It's pictured in no travel magazines because it can't be photographed. But in this new dispensation, believers are much more closely related to heaven than to the world because, through the Spirit, we have become the permanent dwelling-place of God.

Which is not to say that the Holy Spirit has simply abandoned those who don't believe. There's not an artist in this world whose powers aren't animated by the Spirit's working. There's not a computer genius anywhere on the globe who doesn't receive her creativity from the operation of the

Holy Ghost. Look, this isn't hard to understand: God is everywhere, and inasmuch as he is in three persons, he operates as the Holy Spirit in everything from nuclear medicine to landfill management. The world is not without the Spirit, not for a minute.

That people pooh-pooh the Holy Spirit is not a mark of God's absence in their lives, but an indication of their rejection of his Spirit. That rejection does not bode well for their eternal futures.

But to those who believe, the Holy Spirit's presence is vital proof of God's coming to dwell with us. He has touched us, and in the deepest life of our soul, he has established a bond whereby, in the heart of our very being—in our senses, our perceptions, and our feelings—we know his presence. That assurance has nothing to do with gifts or talents; the most creative can be deprived, while the least cultured or educated can know very deeply the Holy Spirit's presence.

Now our having the Holy Spirit in this new dispensation does not create the same state we will reach in God someday. That heavenly reality will be pure enjoyment; we'll carry nothing of our sin, not even a memory. But here, even with the Holy Spirit in our hearts, we still know clearly that we are in the process of undergoing divine surgery. We still know our own blindness, our ignorance, our temptations, and our unworthiness. But, in us, the Holy Spirit operates against our sin every morning and afternoon and evening of our lives. He remains our comforter.

This really is our condition: we sink away into the misery of sin too easily, yet we know the working of the Holy Spirit, holding us up against that descent.

And the glory is this—he doesn't quit, even when we fall. The indication of his eternal persistence with those who are his own, a persistence we know by his great love, is that God Almighty, by way of his indwelling Spirit, does not simply stop in for a visit once in a while, but that he is forever with us. Forever. He will not depart. He won't quit.

To know that from the center of our being is bliss. It is the greatest wealth we can have.

ACQUAINT NOW
THYSELF WITH HIM

Acquaint now thyself with him, and be at peace:
thereby good shall come unto thee.
—Job 22:21

I t's an odd admonition, isn't it?—"acquaint yourself with God." It implies estrangement or distance. If someone were to tell any one of us to "acquaint yourself with God," we'd likely take offense.

Kids from broken homes can be told to get acquainted with a step-dad or mom. That makes some sense. And we can all be advised to acquaint ourselves with new people—in the office, in the church, in the school. It's good advice. In fact, it's necessary. If we want to get along with new relatives or friends, we've got to accustom ourselves to their ways. Maybe they're hard of hearing, or they talk too much, or they let the kids get away with murder. Hey, if we want to get along, we've got to adjust, to hold something back in ourselves . . . sometimes, the desire to scream. Acquainting ourselves with others almost always means putting on some restraints for the sake of getting along.

Not so with God. If something strikes us strange in the Lord's ways, it's our perceptions that are badly wired. If we were what we should be, we'd never consider his ways odd. But sin scrambles everything. The problem is our unbelief.

Unbelief, you see, is quite reasonable, and it happens in understandable steps. First, we look at life and speak almost reverently of impenetrable mysteries and problems that defy human understanding. Then, we begin to doubt whether what is revealed to us is accurate; it might be instead merely conditioned by time or be, by modern standards, eccentric. We question the Word first, then God. And here's where unbelief ends, always: we begin to understand and interpret life by our standards, not God's. Our belief about God becomes so completely changed that he appears only where our ideas allow him.

What we've done thereby is completely reversed the order of creation. In essence, we've become atheists because God is no more than our own construction.

Today, every fundamental conception about God—creation, the fall, the work of atonement, life after death, and the last judgment—has been rejected by science, made laughable in the public square, banished from education, and tabooed as topics of conversation among serious-minded people. The worldview of unbelief has much more credence today than the worldview of belief.

For that reason, we need to acquaint ourselves with God. We need to break our ties to the wisdom of the world and enter again with all our senses and ponderings of the heart into the most holy thoughts of God.

In no single area is that adjustment more difficult than in the area of human suffering. In life, bad things happen to good people; conversely, good things happen to bad people. That makes no sense to our human understanding. We can understand a tyrant who doles out blessings to dastardly villains; but it's hard to comprehend horrors like disease and untimely death, what we sometimes call "acts of God," when they come to God's faithful.

But central to our acquainting ourselves with God is Jesus Christ, who suffered more than anyone else ever did. Listen to this: for God so loved the world that he gave his only begotten Son. Jesus Christ was the most godly. He stood outside of sin. He was the best among the children of men, the Son of God. And yet, he suffered most. From his death, our soul's medicine streamed like manna from heaven to cure our ills.

In the cross lies the wisdom of God. Acquaint yourself with this: those who want to understand suffering need to know the dire suffering of Jesus Christ the Lord and understand thereby that God appoints priests and priestesses in the sacrament of suffering, chooses those who, like Christ, will deliver the medicine for sin to ease the ills of his people. Suffering, as Paul says, builds character, perseverance, and hope.

We are a people, not simply a motley crew of individuals. We are humankind. Blessed are those individuals who serve the family with their suffering. They truly serve not only their neighbors but their King. Their assured reward is eternal joy.

A CANDLE OF
THE LORD

The spirit of man is the candle of the LORD,
searching all the inward parts of the belly.
—Proverbs 20:27

When a mother nurses her baby, something beyond words is communicated. A bond is established by eye contact, by cooing and baby talk, by the warmth of mutually close and loving bodies. The child reads the tenderness of sheltering love in the face of her mother, and what happens between them begins a relationship for life, even though no ideas are shared and no words pass between them.

Yet that communion is conscious, not unconscious. The child somehow knows that what she is receiving is love, just as the mother understands perfectly what she feels for her child. In the process, what's created between them is a bond that is much deeper than shared knowledge and is not altogether unlike the relationship created between God and his people when we understand and cultivate his nearness to us.

If we keep the mother and child in mind, then it's easy to understand why being near unto God isn't something that lapses or dissipates when we're suffering, say, fever tantrums or when we're under anesthetic. When we faint or when we sleep, God doesn't leave us. Like our sight during sleep, it may not be operative but it's not gone.

All of that is important inasmuch as it makes vivid once again that our nearness to God goes far deeper than our own understanding of that relationship. Knowing God means becoming aware of his presence; it's a perceiving and feeling that we really cannot simply attribute to our emotions because it's not that fickle. To think of knowing God as simply what we feel would be to fall into a false mysticism. We know what we do about God's nearness because we somehow perceive it within us by the linking of our inner selves to the life of God. It's a whole lot more than emotions.

The Bible's description of what is inside us is not always as clear as we might like. It often speaks collectively about our "innermost parts" yet also at times distinguishes between heart and soul. It may be helpful to think of the two of them together, at least if the verse above is to have much meaning.

Let's call the heart and soul the consciousness, that gift of God, that handiwork of his which he maintains within. It acts like the sun, bringing light to a world that otherwise would be not at all clear to us. Our consciousness shines into our innermost selves so that we can examine and appraise our own most private selves with respect to our relationship to God.

It's obvious that God doesn't need this candle. He has cat's eyes. He sees into darkness as if it weren't there. He sees into our souls without the aid of any extra sense.

But we need this consciousness, this "spirit of man," this "candle of the Lord." It is a gift of God to lighten the darkness of our inner being. By his light we come to know and to evaluate our own "innermost parts."

We create, to be sure, our own light. By our powers of reasoning, by our vivid imaginations, by our creative spirits, we bring some clarity to what otherwise would be life's messes. But our best thinking, like our most creative imaginative play, can be and often is seriously flawed. When we think we've come to understand something perfectly, often enough we mislead ourselves—quite easily, as a matter of fact. No exercise in logic will ever be sufficient to evaluate the state of our own "innermost parts." That job belongs only to the "candle of the Lord," which he gives us and thereby becomes "the spirit of man."

This light doesn't rant and rave or even argue. It doesn't analyze or try to rationalize behavior. The candle of God, our consciousness, merely lays bare whatever is in us. It places the stuff of our selves before the eye of the soul, brings self-knowledge, and surgically removes self-deception.

By his candle, we come to know ourselves—and him—much, much better. It's a process, an understanding we grow into, by his light.

I in Them, and Thou in Me

I in them, and thou in me.
—John 17:23

Even though our mystical union with Christ is absolutely central to faith, even though all the apostles and the greatest leaders of the church throughout history return to that union time and time again, even though Christ's nearness to us is indispensable to our own deep devotion, the temptation we all feel is to stay at the cross and Golgotha and to go no farther. That is fatal to faith.

And it's so easy. The process is simple and understandable. The conscience awakens us to the weight of our own sin, and we begin to fear the judgment. Hell strikes terror in our souls. Then, wonderfully, the knowledge of the cross arises and brings great comfort to our dread. At that moment, we are saved: once we accept the Lord's work on the cross, the requirement of belief has been satisfied. We're home free. We're fully persuaded of the efficacy of Christ's death, so we seal the bargain by accepting him into our lives as our personal Savior.

But if that's where religion ends, the really significant joys of a redeemed life will remain unknown to us. We remain on the level of spiritual egoism. We've escaped from spiritual doom. We dry our sweaty foreheads as if we'd just suffered a very close call. But what is missing is the growth of the life of the soul, something that can be understood only when we understand fully the nature of Christ's work.

He is our Mediator, after all. Mediators have a role to play; they bring us to something else. Christ, as our Mediator, brings us to the Father. To be near unto God is to know the Father with a child's confidence, to know his nearness with conviction, and then to abide in that nearness for a lifetime and to serve him even more fully in the Father-house above on the day we leave this earth.

If we confine our interests to our own soul and have no greater desire to be numbered with God's people, our own spiritual progress may well be arrested, if not aborted. We need to be given to the Father by the hands of our Mediator, Jesus Christ. Listen to the whole idea Christ brings to the Father: "And the glory which thou gavest me I have given them; that they may be one in us, even as we are one: I in them, and thou in me, that they may be made perfect in one; and that the world may know that thou hast sent me, and hast loved them, as thou hast loved me" (John 17:22-23).

Piety that lolls in its own emotions or glories in its own sweet bliss lacks power and animation. What's more, Christ himself never desired any other task than to bring us to the Father. When one knows Christ's wonderful atonement, it's frightfully easy to create a Christ-cult, a religion that honors Jesus Christ at the expense of the Father. That faith doesn't really honor Christ at all. It's something he wouldn't have wanted himself.

This isn't an easy distinction, but understanding it is crucial. The work of atonement is performed by Christ, not by the Father. He is our Mediator. But the end and purpose of Christ's work is to bring us to something else—to bring us near unto God.

And that nearness is difficult to describe with words. The company of believers God creates by bringing us near unto him is unlike any other organization. We don't wear similar T-shirts or sing the same songs. We don't apply for membership or tailor ourselves to fit company policies. We are appointed by God and, miraculous as it sounds, even a child who has never spoken the word "God" can belong.

What's more, we aren't all alike. We're not chosen by beauty, wisdom, integrity, or our investment portfolios. If we had our way, we'd likely not choose the same folks that God chooses. But with the whole motley crew, we are under Christ, our living Head, who gives us the glow of love. Under his mediating hand we come near unto God, who assures us of eternity and guarantees the highest accomplishment of our existence, all for his own honor and glory.

Christ is the means to that end, not the end itself. Christ ties the knot that links us eternally with the Father. "I in them, and thou in me."

THE SPIRIT RESTETH
UPON YOU

*If ye be reproached for the name of Christ, happy are ye; for the
spirit of glory and of God resteth upon you.*
—1 Peter 4:14

Who can forget the picture of Stephen, on his knees, stones and
rocks already slamming into his body, as he asks forgiveness of
those who are, at that moment, killing him? Martyrdom is memorable
and, in its own way, beautiful.

But even though there have been hundreds and thousands of martyrs
for Christ's sake throughout history, real bloodletting martyrdom is somewhat rare. The kind of suffering for Christ's sake that isn't rare, but still is
persecution, is the mockery and scorn that almost all believers suffer at
some time in their lives at the hands of an unbelieving world. Christ's
words at the end of the Beatitudes are worth remembering: "Blessed are
ye, when men shall revile you, and persecute you, and shall say all manner
of evil against you falsely, for my sake" (Matt. 5:11). Nothing in that
promise calls us to militant action, but Jesus does offer certain relief to victims of abuse suffered for his sake.

The desire to suffer for Christ has affected many throughout the ages.
Sometimes Christians can be overzealous in their pursuit of righteousness. Sometimes Christians seem almost loveless in their enthusiasm.
Sometimes believers are downright hypocritical, and their professions of
faith are horribly disfigured as a result.

Sometimes zeal is practiced for self, not God. When that happens,
other believers, people who should be on our side, deliberately take the

opposite stance, since they feel that we're taking Christ's name for a cause more ours than his. That disfigures him too.

But don't be mistaken. If we think that being a Christian means being soft and sweet as a teddy bear, we're dead wrong. Christians are capable of tremendous charity and philanthropy; we can be lovingly honest and upright. But if we only do that of which the world approves, then the distinctive quality of faith isn't in us. Think of the apostles who never did anything unethical, yet were hounded to the death for their faith alone.

How we act as Christians depends significantly on our being near unto God. When we are close, the scorn and abuse of the world is really directed at him, not us. We are the victims of God-hatred because we have him in our hearts, not for our own sake.

The world is full of hatred—witness Cain and Abel. But we're not talking here about the kind of hatred satisfied by someone else's attaining love or money or power. What we're talking about is hatred we receive, plain and simple, from God in us.

The desire for rights and freedoms, the will to be lord and master of one's own life, the need to recognize no authority but self, the yearning to be as God—even to be God—is the pride-drenched wish of all humankind. Satan started the whole mess, and he infected humanity with his disease. Because Christianity preaches selflessness, it is always at odds with the pride that infects our souls. Faith bends the knee; sin straightens it angrily.

To be near unto God is a condition so wonderful that we sometimes feel a desire to pull away from the world and its enmity. But that's wrong. Listen to the words of Christ: "I pray not that thou shouldest take them out of the world, but that thou shouldest keep them from the evil" (John 17:15).

When we are near to God, scorn and contempt will naturally follow, not because of who we are but because of *whose* we are. In that nearness is the promise of the beatitude, the promise of blessedness.

We should never court martyrdom. No one should desire the martyr's crown or incite the world to scorn us or him. But when we are persecuted for righteousness' sake, then Jesus says, we are blessed—and not just in the hereafter, but in the very teeth of a world that hates the truth of the gospel of Christ. His spirit rests upon us graciously in our suffering.

ONE AFTER THIS
MANNER AND
ANOTHER AFTER THAT

But every man hath his proper gift of God,
one after this manner, and another after that.
—1 Corinthians 7:7

Dog: a domesticated, quadruped carnivore, adorned with fur, a tail (sometimes), and given to bark (some worse than others); often proudly loyal and even slavish (from a cat's point of view anyway).

Even though any mention of the word *dog* brings an immediate picture to everyone's imagination, each image is different. Ones tent has to be pretty wide to admit a German shepherd and a dachshund in the same area. Cockers are known for their floppy ears, dobermans for their ferocity, and English sheepdogs for their uncanny ability as shepherds. But they're all dogs.

Everywhere in creation we see the same kind of diversity. You want copies, go to a Xerox. You want differences, look at life. No two roses are the same; no two fingerprints; no two elms, wood ducks, earthworms, mountain ranges, landscapes, clouds, or coastlines. And no two believers. Unanimity is a quality diligently sought on an assembly line but unavailable in life.

And yet Christians—even good Christians—fall victim to a desire for the unnatural condition of sameness. Somewhere at bottom, pride may be the cause; but more likely the desire to turn out Christians as stiffly patterned as Christmas cookies emerges from motives that are, in intent, good and sweet.

Here's what happens. We earnestly seek the Lord. We look to other Christians for patterns of behavior, other Christians we identify as more mature in the faith, as practiced believers, as people we might even envy for their faith. Then we grow. Slowly but surely, and individually, we come to a deeper and richer walk with God. We feel his presence daily. Our lives become blessed, and we know it.

In our joy at having arrived, we look back at the path we've taken and, out of a sincere desire for the benefit of others, direct any who are searching toward the path we've taken. We've developed an impression of what a Christian should be, and a certain species of piety becomes, for us at least, the most desirable. We begin to assume that Christians who don't pray with their hands raised aren't really praying. We start to believe that every Christian must read Aristotle, Calvin, or even Kuyper. We prescribe *the* path to God. We think we can do the Word's work—drawing maps to grace. Our way becomes God's way.

It happens. And it happens regularly. And even though the intent is wonderful, the practice is evil. God's children should glory in their liberty, in their differences. Just as no two fingerprints are alike, no two believers are formed by God in exactly the same way. Our diversity is our strength.

But liberty isn't license. Even though every bird in the woods sings a uniquely different song, their warbling is God's gift and not their own.

We are—each of us—an intricately designed piece of work, an almost impossible conglomeration of diverse, individual forces: the powers of our ancestry, the sensitivity of our nerves, the vigor of our imagination, and the depth of our understanding. And more. We are formed by the way our hearts are strung, by our disposition, our inclinations and sympathies, the range of our consciousness, our susceptibility to emotions and sensations, our education, our environment, and our calling. All of these put a stamp on us and our spirituality.

What all of this forms is a uniqueness created by the Holy Spirit, not just a garment we wear through life, but what we are. Each of us has his or her own beauty, and only when our walk with God is uniquely ours will we be free and spirited.

Each of us come near unto God in a particular, peculiar, and personal way, the way God has written up long before we were born. Just as a mother knows her children by their voices, God knows us by the individual voice he has himself created and elicited from our very souls.

AFTER THE FIRE A STILL SMALL VOICE

But the LORD was not in the fire:
and after the fire a still small voice.
—1 King 19:12

Approach some wonderful old grandmother sometime and ask her about her life. What she's likely to give you is a testimony that's many chapters long, a testimony punctuated heavily by God's presence.

But what she's also likely to reveal is that the nature of God's presence differed slightly throughout her life. In her childhood, God may have seemed the very personification of joy and happiness. As a teenager, she might well have gone to him for comfort in the stress of trying to find herself and her way. As a young mother, teaching her children the Bible stories she learned herself, she probably came to understand him much more fully than she'd ever imagined. Now, as a senior citizen, she might testify that he is closer than he's ever been before.

Elijah saw the Lord in radically different ways. Think of the public drama on Mt. Carmel—thunder and lightning, fire in the middle of a cloudburst, God's flintlike hand on display before hundreds of rubber-necked gawkers. Elijah must have been stunned to see such a spectacle of glory, even though he was confident God would answer his prayers.

Yet, just a short time later, after more thunder and even an earthquake, the Bible tells us that God took a completely different voice. After the fireworks came "a still small voice."

Each of us is decidedly different from each other. That's clear. But what we can learn from the elderly and from Elijah's story is that even in the journey of our own lives, God comes to us in different ways. He knows our needs in every period of life and meets them. Those who try to standard-ize a single approach to God, make one way *the* way, not only discount our individual differences but limit God's hand. Attempts to universalize the Christian experience are not only bound for failure; they're plain sin.

When adults push adult piety onto kids, their children's growth will be checked, if not choked. Parents who try to raise their kids as if they weren't any different from each other risk perverting what would otherwise flour-ish gloriously. The Son of God, like the sun in the heavens, works his way individually on the souls he brings to God.

Generally speaking, men and women are different. Feelings, talents, perceptions, powers are often not the same. But who would dare to say that the lily is somehow less important than the palm tree? In nature, all kinds of beauty prosper spectacularly.

Many feel that the soul-life of women is not the same as the soul-life of men. If that's true, then when men require a male style of faith from women, they limit both women and God's own beneficence. But the same is true for women.

In marriage, when the degree of nearness to God differs between spouses, the godly wife who wants her husband to come to God can eas-ily subvert any possibility of that happening if she pushes her spiritual ways at him. And it's just as true in the opposite direction. God comes to all of us differently.

Even in churches, God tends his people differently. At times, the church must mount unsparing resistance against unbelief. But when con-flict subsides and peace returns, the work changes to a quiet pursuit of God's kingdom. Sometimes men, seemingly more equipped to fight, are better at war than peace; once they fall into a period of relative rest, they lose spirituality quite quickly.

What's at issue here is our individual differences. It's fatal to think we're all alike.

Sometimes in confrontation, sometimes in peace, sometimes in moments of quiet meditation, and sometimes in the messy busyness of our lives, God's nearness is vital, animating, and vigorous. The seasons of his love are much like the seasons of the year—if you know only summer, your sensibilities are impoverished. The believer who adjusts herself to the changes that God brings is the wealthy child of the wealthy Father in heaven.

THOU DIDST MAKE ME HOPE

Thou didst make me hope when
I was upon my mother's breasts.
—Psalm 22:9

W e have, in the Scripture, three remarkably similar testimonies of God's eternal designs. Paul describes God's work this way: "it pleased God, *who separated me from my mother's womb*, and called me by his grace, to reveal his Son in me" (Gal. 1:15-16).

Jeremiah, repeating God's words, testifies this way: "*Before I formed thee in the belly*, I knew thee; and *before thou camest forth out of the womb* I sanctified thee" (Jer. 1:5). David's explanation of God's hand in his life is remarkably similar: "*But thou art he that took me out of the womb: thou didst make me hope when I was upon my mother's breasts. I was cast upon thee from the womb: thou art my God from my mother's belly*" (Ps. 22:9-10).

All three writers glory in God's hand in their lives already before they were conscious of anything aside from their own most immediate and fundamental needs.

Listen to this praise: "Thou hast covered me in my mother's womb. I will praise thee; for I am fearfully and wonderfully made: marvelous are thy works; and that my soul knoweth right well. My substance was not hid from thee, when I was made in secret, and curiously wrought in the lowest parts of the earth. Thine eyes did see my substance, yet being unperfect; and in thy book all my members were written, which in continuance were fashioned, when as yet there was none of them" (Ps. 139:13-16).

What David gives us is generic praise, not personal testimony. What he wishes to do is praise God for the way he has fashioned *all* of his children from conception and even before. It's not just David's story. It's all of ours.

These passages illustrate the elaborate plan and design that God has for each of us. So detailed in craft and strategy is that plan that its purposes are already set in the very physiology of our individual lives. God has planted the seeds of our personal faith in our DNA. He's set his plan for us in our genetic structures. We are each his in unique ways. He does not create clones. Just as hair color, eye color, and length of toe and tongue are unique with each of us, so our walk with God is a particular product of that which we are, by nature—by gift of God. The only thing we can be sure of is this: what he's put there, long before we know it, will come to pass.

Therefore, because we're all different, we shouldn't fall victim to the kind of spiritual covetousness that occurs when we wish we were someone else. If fellow believers testify to the way they've experienced God—by going to some special retreat or singing with closed eyes or taking communion in a secret circle or whatever behavior is somehow emotionally fulfilling—don't assume that if you're not receiving a similar emotional charge from a similar religious experience, that's proof of some sin within you, limiting the range of your spiritual experience. We're all different. We're made uniquely—from birth.

Read Saint Augustine's *Confessions*. Just as every young painter can learn from Rembrandt and Rubens but no one will ever copy the work of those masters, every growing Christian can learn a great deal from Augustine, as well as many others, both ancient and contemporary, who testify boldly to God's work in their lives.

But you can't be Augustine. You can't be Mother Theresa. You can't be Calvin or the saint across the street, because already from birth God Almighty, the Creator of the universe and everything in it—including you and me—engineered a particular path for your life, a path nobody else would walk in exactly the same way.

Like Augustine—and David, Jeremiah, and the apostle Paul—it's our job to work out that salvation, to create our own spiritual existence from that very form of hidden fellowship that is uniquely ours. That's all that's required. None of us will ever be Saint Augustine, nor should we try. We must be what God wants us to be.

We don't have to be slaves to other people's expressions of piety, but we are nonetheless slaves, slaves of righteousness, in everything we do. From the moment of our birth, God has been working his will in each of us uniquely. Take comfort from his care.

Worship Him
that Liveth

The four and twenty elders fall down before him that sat on
the throne, and worship him that liveth for ever and ever.
—Revelation 4:10

What little we know about heaven we take mostly from the book of Revelation, where a passage like this one suggests something of a life that will be ours. What this verse offers us is a sense of unending worship to the Father. But what, really, is worship?

Think about worship in contrast to another act of faith—prayer. Prayer and worship are not the same thing, really, and they certainly are not the same in heaven as on earth. We know that prayer occurs in heaven because Christ assures us that he is praying for us. However, his prayer is a different genre than our own. If the angels pray—and we have no reason to think they don't—their prayers are likely of a different stamp as well.

Why? This world is not our home. Our lives here often seem muddled. The sea of troubles that surround us breaks heavily on our weaknesses. Our prayers seek relief from an endless chain of wants that demand supply. Our very condition compels us to pray, even to beg God for his help and deliverance.

In heaven, the angels likely don't ask the Father for daily bread. They're already busy with worship: "Holy, holy, holy is the Lord of hosts," they sing. "The whole earth is full of his glory." Whatever prayers are offered in heaven are offered for our sake, just as those offered here. On earth, prayer is our most important behavior because through it we seek his face. But in glory, worship is the most vital act.

In principle, prayer and worship come close to being opposites. When we pray, what we want of God is his nearness. We want him to come to us. When we worship, what we want is his acceptance of what we bring. Prayer offers our desire that something come to us from God; worship offers our desire that something from us go to God.

Now the fact of the matter is that, on our own, we don't bring much of value to God Almighty. If every angel's tongue were stilled and every believer's heart muted, the God of glory wouldn't need a thing. He is the only self-sufficient being, the I AM.

A measure of his grace to us, a verification of his love, is that even though he doesn't need us for anything, he takes pleasure in the praise and joy we bring him. Our worship, both alone and in public, begins in this joy that he will accept our thanks for his marvelous love. His receiving our thanks is itself an act of his divine love.

Our worship can be a testimony to unbelievers, as our praise in song can witness to those who don't know him; but worship is not something we do *for* others. It's a holy utterance of the depth of our soul's joy, and at best it can adapt itself only partially to the appreciation or benefit of others. Real worship is the testimony of the human soul.

If it's mechanical, it's not worship. It's real only when the soul loses itself in God, when the soul becomes truly astonished at God's virtues and his acts—and in that astonishment breaks forth into praise in the same way the guitar makes music at the mere brush of a hand.

Now hear this. How many of us pray better than we worship? Most of us, right? More of us know the delight and power of prayer than know, deeply, the joy of worship. And it's easy to see why: prayer is quite frequently a packaged listing of our own wants and needs. We're at the center. But in worship, the *we* gets lost. *We* don't count.

Our thanksgiving should fill the waking moments of our lives, no matter what we're doing. But thanksgiving is only a training school for real worship because our thanks are still rooted in what God has done for us. Real worship glorifies God's majesty, period.

Every day Islamic believers recite the virtues of Allah from the Koran, with little reference to themselves. On that score, we don't do as well. We teach our children to pray, don't we? But do we teach them to worship?

And yet it's clear from the angels in glory that nothing brings our souls so near unto God as our worship.

THE BODY IS NOT ONE MEMBER, BUT MANY

For the body is not one member, but many.
—1 Corinthians 12:14

Christ is King, not merely of Zion, his heavenly residence, and not only of the creation that God the Father fashioned from dust before time began. As King, Christ rules over both of those domains, but that is not the extent of his kingdom. He is, as we know, also the King of our lives. We are his subjects, his people.

Christ's relationship to us isn't at all simple. Take a run through his job description for a moment, and see for yourself. Christ is our Savior, rescuing us from the oppressive tonnage of our sin; he is our protector, keeping us safe from the peril all around us; he is our shepherd, caring and guiding, feeding and leading us. What's more, he is *the* example of how to live our lives.

And more. He's our lawyer, right there at the Father's side, arguing our case. And he's our king, a role that has its own list of functions and tasks.

Even though this is not a laughing matter, Christ's description is so preposterous that it's something of a joke: Christ the King is a lamb, the paradoxical union of self-effacement and dominion, an unbelievable metaphorical one-two punch. At once, he is a lamb, maybe the lowest form of quadraped life, an animal thought by all accounts to be significantly lacking in street smarts; but he is also, of all things, a King, that human role traditionally reserved only for the best and brightest. What a combination! What a Savior!

We err when we think of Christ's kingship as if that image were something drawn from the darkest years of the medieval age. We shouldn't think of him as some pompous potentate in a faraway castle who spends most of his hours dabbling in court politics and only tangentially thinking about the rude swains, his subjects, off in some faraway field plowing the ground to make money enough to pay his family's taxes.

While Christ does occupy a far-off residence (far more magnificent than anything on Palm Beach); and while he has his business to attend there; and while we do, in fact, his work, the similarity between an old tarnished image of a distracted king and Christ's own divine kingship is very, very slight.

To understand it best, we need to think of the terms *head*, *lord*, and *king* as very much linked in our relationship to him. Because he is our *head*, he is part of who we are. The same blood flows through the body as the head, after all. We are his, not simply because we are his possessions, but because we are actually intimately part of him—as he is of us. We are made of the same stuff—hard as that is to believe, undeserving as we are.

Because he does own us, however, he is our Lord too. We are his property. With his blood, we were purchased from Satan's kingdom. And because we are his—and we are literally him—he is also our King. It is his law that rules our lives now that we have become his people.

The body of Christ is an organism—like the human body, like a linden tree, like a porpoise, like anything that lives. But it's also an organization, like the state or a corporation or an association of tool-and-die machinists. It's a whole made up of many parts, a collective noun, a unit at which Christ rules as head, as king. Christ himself used an image from nature to define the relationship—I am the vine, he said, and you are the branches (John 15:1). We function as a whole, as an organism.

Don't ever think that Christ sits in some faraway place doodling while the affairs of this world spin around madly, waiting for someone to bring order to the chaos. It's not that way. His kingship isn't simply dealt to us; we're not the minions of a fat-cat king.

The fact is, as parts of the body we are intimately connected with him—because he is our head. One Spirit animates us all, just as one blood courses through our veins. Therefore, today, every single movement of Christ the King affects us. His stirring makes us, his own limbs, shake and move; his direction prompts us to build or tear down. He is our King, and he moves us as he loves and owns us, his own body.

LORD, TEACH
US TO PRAY

*One of his disciples said unto him, Lord, teach
us to pray, as John also taught his disciples.*
—Luke 11:1

Even though at times we do it poorly, there's no escaping the fact
that every believer *must* pray. One cannot come near to God without prayer. It requires clarity, urgency, and readiness of soul. And it's never
simply crafted. If it's artifice, it's not prayer.

And yet prayer is something learned. Even the disciples, who followed
Jesus every day, didn't know exactly how to do it. "Lord, teach us to pray,"
they asked. When he answered, Christ didn't say, "Do it after this fashion."
What he told them was this: "When you pray, say. . . ." He gave them the
very words in a form that seems specially designed for groups. The pronoun *our* is used throughout: our Father, our daily bread, our sins. For centuries, that prayer has been used in worship.

Scottish reformers, fervent about ridding the church of its formalism,
stopped using the Lord's Prayer in worship. To the Scots, the Lord's
Prayer seemed canned, ritualistic, meaningless repetition. Prayer reaches
its highest form when, free from every bit of formality, it rises from the
depths of the soul on the wings of the Spirit and comes before God the
Father in holy and consecrated language. When we offer that kind of
prayer, the words of the Lord's Prayer may not be adequately specific for
our needs.

Most of us know that kind of intense prayer because in our own lives
those prayers are memorable to us. But few of us experience that kind of
fervency every day. It's equally unlikely that every single Sunday of the

year someone from the congregation can reach that level of intensity. While such vigor may be the mountaintop, above the tree line there's not much life, really. In public worship, at least, extemporaneous prayer isn't *always* preferable to the Lord's Prayer—or fixed forms in general.

Besides, not all members of an individual church may be seasoned pray-ers. Don't forget that it was Christ's own compatriots who asked how to pray. Obviously, they didn't know how exactly. Christ gave them words we still use.

Vain repetitions are indeed vain. Something is profaned when our minds wander in our most holy acts. But what about singing? It would be something if every song offered in worship were the unique and personal utterance of the individual soul. But if each song were unique, how would we sing together? How would we know the music? And what about Scripture? How many times haven't we heard Psalm 23? Because we know it so well, should it *not* be read?

Minds wander in extemporaneous prayer too. Minds wander during the "Hallelujah" chorus. Minds wander during a dramatic reading of the crucifixion. As commendable as it is to avoid the dry bones of formality, we should remember that when Christ gave his disciples the Lord's Prayer, he used the command form: "When you pray, say. . . ." Doesn't that command rule out our avoidance?

Besides, as everyone knows, certain repetitions feed spirituality—a treasured verse of Scripture, the chorus of "Jesus Loves Me," the hymn sung at a grandma's funeral. While fixed forms can lead to mindless repetition, they are also capable of beautifully enhancing our spirituality. Some people love to read the Bible before personal prayers because the familiar words prepare them for coming near unto God.

Most preachers don't write individual benedictions for the close of the service. Does their repetition of those same words numb and freeze? In many ways, for us to hear them time and time again as we leave the sanctuary is to know that we have been part of an enterprise much bigger than ourselves. We have been part of God's greater and larger family and hearers of those words repeated throughout the world and for as long as his people have come together to worship him.

Sometimes the words of the Lord's Prayer, like so many fixed forms, are the gentle dew of grace that comes only from God Almighty. That prayer is not designed for a showcase. It's given to us for our use. It is the very model for our coming near unto God.

As It Is in Heaven

Thy kingdom come. Thy will be
done in earth, as it is in heaven.
—Matthew 6:10

Coming near unto God is a two-way street: God comes to us, *and* we come to him. It's important to remember that, because if we think that our nearness to him depends only on our strength or fervency—or only on his coming to us—we're sadly mistaken. Often enough in life, he comes to us when we are not even conscious of his being beside us—in our sickness, for example, or when we are just kids. In those times, he can hold us up with his hands without our even being aware of his presence.

But God wants our aspiration to be near unto him. The Lord's Prayer suggests that clearly. When Christ tells us to pray, "Our Father which art in heaven," he wants us to affirm that God's father-character is something other than an earthly father-character. This Father is in heaven, and we need to seek him some place other than in back rooms or front rooms of our lives. We need to come to him where he is.

"Thy will be done on earth, as it is in heaven" implies that we know something about how his will is carried out where he is. This petition suggests clearly our confirmed knowledge of what might be called "spiritual things" or the spiritual world. It simply assumes that we know something about our Father's house, the place where he dwells.

When we die and come to him, we all know God won't be alone, some solitary figure of grandeur in eternity. We all know there are angels and saints in residence in the Father's house. When we die, we'll meet a company, the extended family of God's people.

Isaiah knew that. He even recorded their song: "Holy, holy, holy is the LORD of hosts" (6:3), they sang—and still do. John, on Patmos, records another anthem: "Thou art worthy, O Lord, to receive glory and honor and power" (Rev. 4:11). The psalmist extols the angelic community to glorify God: "Bless the LORD, ye his angels, that excel in strength, that do his commandments, hearkening unto the voice of his word. Bless ye the LORD, all ye his hosts; ye ministers of his, that do his pleasure" (Ps. 103: 20-21).

God's spiritual loyalists exist; where he dwells, he is not alone. But often we don't believe in the reality of angels and saints, nor of their work on our behalf. Perhaps we don't think of them because their spirituality makes us nervous.

And well it might. After all, it's remarkably easy to abuse angels and saints by assigning them a higher status than we should. By making the angels or his saints unnecessary middle agencies between the soul and God, a well-meaning believer's search for angelic fellowship often has drawn him away from the nearness of God instead of leading him into God's holy presence.

When that happens, a good dose of spiritual sobriety is needed. So people react against such false worship by avoiding any discussion of a different spiritual reality than what we see ourselves. To avoid one abuse, sometimes people fall into another. But the Lord's Prayer is clear: we should take close note of the reality of angels and saints. In the "Our Father," Jesus gives us a pattern for our prayers that brings our souls, again and again, in touch with this higher spiritual world.

Just as intimate fellowship with those strong in faith and wisdom will enhance our relationship with God, coming into contact with the angels will enhance our holiness, even though it will not wipe out our sin. Our prayers can be carried on the wings of the angels, whose presence in our lives will make it less difficult to lift ourselves up from our lives in the here-and-now and into greater intimacy with God.

We're not free agents, and we're not alone. When we feel we're fighting the battle all by ourselves, we feel something unnatural and fearful. But the fact is, we come to the knowledge of God not alone but "with all the saints."

If fellowship with God's spiritual family will be our joy in glory, why not now? We are, with his saints, one body with Christ as our head. Often on earth we taste so little of this fellowship, even though its work is open to us. Blessed are those who come near unto God with the aid of his spiritual family. They know deeply they are not alone.

STRIVING AGAINST SIN

Ye have not yet resisted unto blood, striving against sin.
—Hebrews 12:4

Concern for our health keeps some of us from smoking or drinking to excess. A desire not to injure our reputation may well keep us from wandering into casinos or porn shops. Some of us avoid throwing away money on silly things simply to remain financially solvent. Some avoid certain activities—say, going to a football game on Sunday—because of prohibitions created by their own particular religious subculture. Profanity may well be frowned upon because it's thought to be improper.

We shouldn't pooh-pooh such motivations. They're valid. As long as sin is restrained, we're all better off, sin itself being contagious, virus-like. We've all heard of copycat crimes. How many of us don't rationalize our own questionable behavior on the basis of having seen someone else—someone we thought more righteous—doing it?

Listen to David's confession in Psalm 51: "Against thee, thee only, have I sinned and done this evil in thy sight: that thou mightest be justified when thou speakest, and be clear when thou judgest" (v. 4). What David recognizes is the genuine nature of sin, its opposition to God. Only when we strive against sin *because* sin opposes God does our striving achieve a holy and higher character. Only when we fight our common enemy with God do we come near to him. It's easy to see why. A common foe always unites. When we fight sin for his sake, we become God's allies. He even supplies the weaponry.

Having said that, however, let's look a bit closer at the nature of our own personal warfare and identify some characteristics of the battles we all face. We have, each of us, some extremely personal sins; the believer who doesn't recognize them in himself is wearing blinders. For some, it's sex; for others, envy. Some of us know our gifts too well and must constantly humble ourselves or be humbled. Some people love to talk and gossip. Others actually love to hate.

For many of us, the battles are fought daily, hourly. We want a better job, a place on the coast, a new wife, a stiff drink. Such battles are primary and important. They demand constant surveillance and strategies. At times, the battle itself is overwhelming.

We shouldn't forget that when our entire arsenal is aimed at keeping ourselves from getting drunk or stepping out on our spouse, we can be victimized by other, lesser sins—treating our kids poorly, for example, or letting our devotional life fall into a mess. Lesser sins have a way of growing like incidental weeds just off the path of those propensities we fight daily.

While that's not okay, it's understandable. If a child is drowning, no rescuer worries about getting wet hair. A more serious wrong will always lessen other problems. But *not* to fight the major problem is to man the towers while leaving the gates wide open. Such tactics make no sense.

The best strategy is to beat the inclination, once and for all—and it can be done. Knowing that our sin can be conquered is the first step in coming near unto God. We can suffer unnecessarily if, for some unknown reason, we think we must fight a particular sin our whole lives. But there's a mystery here. Once the enigmatic character of the human heart reshapes our lust or our envy or our pride into a hated enemy, it often requires that we continue to favor that sin, even if it is as an object of our hate. In a perverse way, we too easily come to treasure our own sin. Maybe we don't practice it anymore, but the act dominates us nonetheless. We fight it for reasons of our own, not for reasons that link that sin to our rejection of God's own character.

What we always need to remember is that our sin is offense against God. Like David, we should never forget the cosmic battle for the sake of our personal enterprise. Sin is not existential. It is real, and God hates it.

We serve God best when we oppose sin for his sake. When we do, we will overcome that sin we've pinpointed as our greatest weakness; and we will, in the battle, come near unto God, our Commander-in-chief. He crowns our work with victory.

LIVE IN PEACE

Be perfect, be of good comfort, be of one mind, live in peace;
and the God of love and peace shall be with you.
—2 Corinthians 13:11

Long ago, church bells regularly rang out over most European countries, reminding people hourly of God's reality. Years ago, when the Reformers did business, transactions as ordinary as rental agreements began by invoking God's name, so committed were those people to recognizing religion in life. In Islamic countries today, civil law is drawn from the pages of the Koran, and not a day passes without a break for prayer. Such zeal can create problems, of course; but nonetheless it seems that coming near unto God is more difficult when very few cultural signals and prompts remind us of his reality.

Sometimes one wonders if the church of Christ today really understands the effort necessary to keep believers near unto God. Church bells are silent today, so we need to find new ways to remind ourselves to search for God's own face.

The apostle says that at least one means to be near unto God is to "live in peace." And yet, it seems that the church is as continually shaken by division and dissension as is the world. Even believers are at war constantly.

What the apostle doesn't say is that believers must always agree. That won't happen. Our sin makes divisions almost inevitable. Paul himself never kept to the sidelines during contentions in the early church. He always weighed in with his opinion.

Whenever disagreements of significant substance arise, each of us is pulled in two different directions. On one hand, we want to keep a civil tongue, to argue in love and respect, and to keep from alienating our antagonists. On the other hand, we'd love to lob grenades, to flame away at the opposition.

It doesn't take a genius to know that the first way creates love and peace; the second, bitterness and anger. We need God's grace to act on that knowledge—to do good and to love, even in disagreement.

What is true in church divisions is just as true when divisions arise within the family. If respect and kindness are shown, love can flourish despite differences. But too many families today are torn in half by disagreements perforated by gunfire, rather than mended by kindness and mutual respect.

Let's be honest. In our world, as in our families and in our churches, there really is no peace. Wars and rumors of wars abound, don't they? How many families are as perfect as those pictured in fifties sitcoms? We all wrangle and wrestle and have our off days.

Creating an atmosphere of love, the apostle says, will not only cut down on hostility and outright anger, but it will bring us closer to God at the very same time. That's the promise. And the reason is simple. When gunfire echoes in our most intimate circles, it's almost impossible to be near unto God. When the atmosphere is highly charged, lightning strikes all over the land. In those moments, it's easier to pull out the stops of the basest human emotions than to stay close to God's face. A gentle mind is a blessing to a family, a church, and a community; similarly, a deeply spiteful person pollutes everything around him.

Dispensing love instead of gall becomes easier when it's practiced. Once we learn to curb our excesses, we find it easier to act that way again and again and again.

But don't be fooled. We're not talking about cheap appeasement. Those who are afraid to enter the fight do not gain a dime's worth of righteousness. Indifference can be plain and simple cowardice.

In this world, there won't be an abundance of rose gardens. It's tough for us simply to get along. Nonetheless, an atmosphere of love and peace brings us near unto God—that's the promise. And that's reason enough to avoid strife and unrest. Hostility draws us away from him who loves us most. It's that plain and that simple.

A DECEIVED HEART

A deceived heart has turned him aside.
—Isaiah 44:20

Most of us have had the unpleasant experience of coming to the end of the day and realizing that all day long God was, for all practical purposes, out of sight and out of mind. When that happens, invariably we ask ourselves the question, why?

The answer is simple. We're too busy. Like an overused electrical outlet, our attention is overwhelmed by a hundred appliances seeking to draw our energy. We've just got too much going on. That's how we answer the question.

That's hooey. God doesn't stand outside of our lives, like some lakeside cottage waiting, once or twice a year, to divert our attention from the cares of our workaday world. The alienation we feel from God in the middle of our lives is not a result of our busyness, but our sin. Call a spade, a spade.

We can't tithe our attention to God. If we tell ourselves that a tenth of our day will be spent in prayer, we're looking at the whole relationship wrong. We're just as misguided if we say that 90 percent of our time should belong to God, 10 percent to this world. God isn't a commodity, a single frame in a game of bowling. God is in everything. If we're not seeing him, we're simply not looking.

Adam told God he knew the problem. It was Eve. Eve said it was the serpent. They were both lying. In a similar fashion, we blame our wandering on the serpent of this world—on our busyness, our work, our commitment to our children, or our church work. Some of us claim what keeps us from God is a backache, a headache, or some other infirmity.

And then along comes Isaiah with this striking charge against all of us: "A deceived heart hath turned him aside" (44:20).

Isaiah says we fashion our own idols. He claims we cut that which we worship out of the world as if it were a tree branch. We carefully extract the knots, carve that chunk of wood to a shape that pleases us, then plane it and sand it smooth, lay a coat of polyurethane over it to make it shine, and set this creation of ours in the center of our lives. It's an idol.

But Isaiah says the wooden image itself is not the sin. It's the spirit that went into its making. In our fascination with cutting and molding and shaping and carving and polishing, we lose all sight of our own idolatry. We've been turned so far around the bend and away from God that we don't understand we have self-deception right there in our hands. We are obsessed by what we've done. That's what Isaiah says.

He's not wrong. We all recognize the obsessed by their cold stare, by their seeming indifference to polite conversation, or by their tightly focused life. Something holds their attention with such force that they become fanatic. We can guess the nature of their conversation the moment we spot them coming our way. Maybe it's money. Maybe it's pleasure. Maybe it's some form of art or some perplexing scientific problem. Maybe it's sports or gossip or politics. Maybe it's simply their work. But we recognize obsession.

The sad fact is that we're all, in part, guilty of burying ourselves in our work—even believers. No man or woman can serve two masters, the Bible says; yet we all feel the propensity to try to live two lives, one sacred and one secular. To know the rise of the Holy Spirit within us is to feel the urgent desire that goes out after God in everything we do, not just some things. When we come to know God, we don't need to repress anything from our attention, because with the Holy Spirit's encouragement we live in constant proximity to the Lord God Almighty.

When you come to the end of the day and suddenly tell yourself that you didn't really consider your God since early morning (or even the night before), don't blame busyness. Study your heart and recognize the idols there, idols you've built with your own hands.

The only truth that counts, really, is the question asked by the apostle Paul (Gal. 2:20): Don't you understand that Christ is in you? Believe it. ▨

WHATSOEVER YE DO

And whatsoever ye do, do it heartily, as to the Lord.
—Colossians 3:23

The God of heaven and earth does not want Sunday Christians. The moment we segment our lives into realms that are sacred and secular, we blaspheme the Creator of all that we have and are. In the Christian life, there can be no separateness, no division; and if you doubt that for a moment, just listen to Scripture: "Pray without ceasing"; "Rejoice in the Lord alway"; "Whatsoever ye do, do it heartily, as to the Lord" (1 Thess. 5:17; Phil. 4:4; Col. 3:23).

Scripture takes no hostages here. It demands all or nothing. We cut no deals and do no bargaining. God takes pleasure only in the entirety of our lives, not simply in our Sundays. The divisions we construct in our lives hurt us and rob God of his due.

Some devote too much of their time to their religion and thereby mess up their families. Some devote too much of their time to things of this world and destroy their souls. We can't give God our souls and still dole out segments elsewhere. Can't be done.

Preachers and plumbers aren't any different. What God requires of them each is the same: not a dime's less than everything. Missionaries are no more holy than factory workers or soccer players or the unemployed. Life, lived near unto God, is holy service. Granted, pastors may likely be busier with holy things and thereby enjoy a greater privilege—for which they will be accountable. And while it's undeniable that maintaining worship at the busy stock market or in a kitchen full of bawling kids is more difficult than dealing moment by moment with matters of the faith, we all know that God will provide strength and comfort for all of his children. What almost every pastor learns early in his ministry is that there are those in the church, often very ordinary people, whose simple faith radiates God's grace and shines in the darkness like an awesome planet.

But because we are so defective, certain conventions of the Christian life draw us into separating life from faith. While it's wrong to center all of one's spirituality on a single day of the week, the Sabbath remains something special. Although we are called to nearness every hour of every day, that nearness is simply not always possible. Therefore, we need special times for prayer and worship and thanksgiving. In the Jerusalem above, there will be no Sunday worship or Christian music because all of life will be praise and glory.

Our faith will shine every moment of the day when we truly believe that our God is the Almighty, the Creator of heaven and earth. When we come to understand that all things were created by his hand, then we will see him in everything around us—in our joys and our trials, in our warmest smiles and stiffest headaches. All of life can be worship when we come to know that all of life is his. Nothing in our personal lives, our family lives, our professional lives, or our recreational lives can be separate from the world he made.

Only sin separates. Sin divides, marginalizes, discriminates, breaks up fellowship with him and with others, and throws us back on our own decrepit devices.

But as for the rest of living, whether you do art, bus tables, lay concrete, clean toilets, bring up kids, care for the elderly, perform brain surgery, pump gas, clean teeth, play football, or shine shoes—no matter what you do—do it to his honor and glory. After all, our life is a whole, the component parts of which—play, duty, leisure—must be wrapped in our love like a present, then laid at the feet of our God.

When all of life is holy service, then we are near unto God. There are no sweet hours of prayer because all of life is nearness. If our every moment is prayer and worship and thanks, then our lifetime is one sweet tribute to the God who loved us so much he sent his Son to keep us from the death we plotted for ourselves.

Devotion can't be mechanical or slavish. Our lives, willingly and gratefully devoted to God, bring praise to his name and joy to the world.

Whatever you do, says the apostle, do it to his glory. That's the whole truth.

HOW EXCELLENT
IS THY NAME

O LORD our Lord, how excellent is thy name in all the earth!
—Psalm 8:9

Have you ever noticed a relationship between the level of devotion people have and their place of habitation? Generally, it seems (and we must be very careful here), rural people seem to be more solid practitioners of their faith than city dwellers, no matter what that faith is—Christian, Islamic, Hindu, or whatever.

Many reasons likely exist for that difference including, simply, a more stoic resistance to change among rural people. Where traditions are more deeply set, they are less casually abandoned. Country people may be less influenced by education, and therefore more deeply rooted in the ways of their ancestors, including the ways of faith.

But we'd be dead wrong to assume that only rural people are devout. Often, the city's difficult tests make certain urban Christians more involved in ministry to the oppressed than their country cousins. But that doesn't change the widely-held perception that the most devout believers of every world religion tend to live in rural areas.

Why? A hailstorm can wipe out a family's future in thirty seconds. Throat-constricting, crop-ravaging drought can devastate a whole region. Whatever seeds one commits to the earth, one commits, really—even with modern agriculture—to God. Country people are simply more obviously dependent on the actual hand of God in nature.

In urban areas, the problems industries face seem to be human problems. How can our supply levels be maintained? What are transportation costs? Do we have sufficient human resources? These are questions asked and answered by and with human beings.

What's more, since the discipline of a public conscience operates more tightly where people know each other well, country people seem more regulated by conscience (some would say repressed!). Organizations are smaller, more intimate; and whether or not it is true, temptations seem less prevalent.

But still, the most important reason for rural solidity of faith is their proximity to nature. If you want to be awed by stars and planets, you've got to escape the city lights. The psalms are full of the wonder of God's glory in creation: the heavens declare his glory; the firmament shows his handiwork; the voice of the Lord is upon the waters; glorious is thy name in all the Earth. Scripture glows with nature's stunning beauty.

We know God's law from the Scriptures. We delight in worship in our churches. We thrill at the love shown us clearly in the gospels. But, if we listen to the confessions, our knowledge of God from his Word is only one side of the coin.

Revelation—God's own story to us—comes in two varieties: his Word and his world. While books can teach us a great deal, and ideas may stretch our imaginations and nurture our intellects, God cannot be visualized by the ideas of our greatest minds nor mimicked by our computer modeling. Small group discussions won't thrill us with a sense of wonder at his presence. Books won't help us feel his majesty.

If you want to sense God's awesome presence, observe the dawn. His staggering power is written in jagged lines of lightning playing against the canvas of a dark sky. If you want to know his immensity, look at stars light-years away in the distant heavens.

God's majesty soars above our petty economies, and when we understand that—when we come to know him in his presence in nature—then we realize we're not the product of bungling human hands, but the glorious high art of the Creator of heaven and earth.

Nature does not teach us the gospel; that good news is the joy of the Bible. But when we sense the Creator of heaven and earth in his own playground, nature itself takes us from human insignificance to divine omnipotence.

In those moments, we are brought into his presence and thereby much nearer to God, the high and lofty Lord of all—a God who yet, amazing as it seems, loves us.

Thou Triest Mine Heart that It Is with Thee

*But thou, O L*ORD*, knowest me: thou*
hast seen me, and tried mine heart toward thee.
—Jeremiah 12:3

I f you want to know how deep our sinful condition goes, try to list what we'll call the indiscretions we all commit daily—the old bitterness we can't kick, the way we raise our chin in arrogance, the moments our tongues get away from us. Often, our little sins don't even register with us. Maybe we think of them an hour later; maybe not.

While those trifling dishonesties stain our character and irritate our relationship to God, they don't, by themselves, prevent us from coming near to him. That we commit "little" sins without recognizing them is an indication of how fallen our natures are; but those "little" sins do not banish us from God.

This is risky language, but let's pursue the idea: it's the "big" sins that keep God at a horrifying distance. What do we mean by a "big" sin? This kind: we know very well that what we're about to do is something unequivocally wrong, but the urge and desire expands like a hot-air balloon in our conscious mind and inflates so greatly that the only relief is to act—even though we know full well we shouldn't. Headstrong, we wade into trouble.

What's the result? Bone-chilling fear of God. Like Adam and Eve, we run for cover because we knew right from the start that this oh-so-good enterprise of ours would trigger God's anger. But we did it anyway. And now we know an eternity of separation lies between us. We feel battered and bruised by our tumble from grace, unable to stand, and incapable of coming near—so we hide.

In Psalm 32, David says that as a result of his sin, he acted like a teenager and didn't say a word to God. But his silence only resulted in further alienation. When he kept silent, he confesses, God's hand was heavy upon him.

By simply knowing that his silence was counterproductive, David begins to understand the next step: to open up to God is much preferable. "I said, I will confess my transgressions unto the LORD" (Ps. 32:5).

Just like that, the separation he'd engineered is behind him. Just like that, he breaks into song. "For this shall every one that is godly pray unto thee in a time when thou mayest be found" (v. 6).

David's antidote is the only effective medicine against the kinds of "big" sins we're considering here. When we deliberately fall and when, as a result, we want nothing more than to hide from God, our silence only increases our anxiety and more completely dissolves our relationship with him.

We've got to speak up, even though it's painful—and it is. Confessing sin is humble pie of the absolute worst taste. It is violence against our pride. Bringing our transgressions before the Lord means suffering his anger. But it also promises forgiveness. The effects of confession are really shocking, as David says. Something melts in the soul, and liberation, redemption, and reconciliation come a'marching in, just like that. God comes near unto us, maybe even nearer than he's ever been. It happens. Trust David. Trust God.

And of course God knows all of this. Listen to Jeremiah: "But thou, O LORD, knowest me: thou hast seen me, and tried mine heart toward thee" (12:3). When we break guilty silence, it's not news to the Lord God Almighty.

In every moment of our lives, we have choices. We face two paths—the way of the Lord or the way of Satan. It's just that simple. Every time we choose to give ear to Satan's prompting, we move away from God. If nearness is really our desire, then our choices have to be God's choices. For when we sign on with the forces of sin, we not only abandon God's side, we do battle with him.

Asking him for forgiveness for our "big" sins—as well as our little ones—is really asking him to look past our dishonor to see that our hearts and minds and souls are, in the deepest depth, not on the side of Satan, but very much with him.

GET THEE BEHIND
ME, SATAN

*Get thee behind me, Satan: . . . for thou savourest not the things
that be of God, but those that be of men.*
—Matthew 16:23

We cringe at the reading of the twenty-second verse of Matthew 16: "Then Peter took [Christ], and began to rebuke him." Imagine the arrogance of the man on whom Christ said he would build his church; imagine him *rebuking*—telling off—Christ, the Son of God.

And yet, when we know the context of the line, Peter's motivations are clear and even sympathetic. Just a few moments after Peter's wonderful confession of faith, "Thou art the Christ, the Son of the living God" (v. 16), Jesus looks at his disciples and narrates his suffering, death, and resurrection.

Still full of enthusiasm for what he's testified, Peter hears the dark news of his Savior's death and shivers to the bone. "Never, Lord," he says, his shoulders squared. "This shall never happen to you!" Typical Peter bravado.

Peter is a strong man, a rock, all right; and his motivation is clear. Ultimately it's love. He will allow this suffering to happen only over his dead body.

What happens next is even more astounding. Jesus turns to Peter. "Get thee behind me, Satan," he says; "thou art an offence unto me: for thou savourest not the things that be of God, but those that be of men" (v. 23). Peter's rebuke is answered in a divine way. Christ actually addresses Peter as "Satan." Peter's love and allegience is answered with words a razor's edge from damnation.

There have been periods in the history of Christianity when good believers dragged Satan into every single difficulty they faced, blaming him for all their troubles. Today, that's hardly the case. Today, we seem to have gone to the opposite extreme. Today, talk of Satan often strikes people as antiquated, as if the devil were the last vestige of the dark ages. Today, we need to remind ourselves again of his cunning, insidious reality.

The story of Peter's love for the Son of God is instructive, not only because Christ blames Satan for what Peter says, but also because the story pinpoints how wily the Prince of Darkness is. Peter would have denied vehemently that his motivations were anything less than martyr-like dedication to the cause; he loved Christ and didn't want to see him suffer. The very idea was so repulsive that his emotions shifted into overkill. "Never," he tells Jesus. "Don't even think it, because it won't happen." No matter how much we love his vigor, Christ understood his enthusiasm for what it was—Satan's deceit.

How often, once some major trauma passes, don't we wonder whether the devil wasn't behind all the pain and sadness? How often, once the smoke clears, don't we have the strong sense that the battles we've waged were with Satan?

Don't forget Peter's story. Never—not in a thousand years—could Peter have guessed that at the moment he thought himself pledging his power most defiantly toward the Son of God, he was, in fact, a card-carrying minion of the Devil of Doom. Love was on Peter's mind, but evil was Satan's intent.

There is much mystery connected with Satan's mode of operation in the world. We know that he exists; after all, the New Testament is full of references to him. Christ's own prayer acknowledges his presence. The devil plays a major role in the pageant-like vision John sees on the isle of Patmos. Satan is real. He is.

We will never fully understand how he operates, however. Criminal minds can be studied and analyzed, but Satan is the Prince of Thieves; often enough he slinks away from our attention only to become, by subterfuge, the star in the dramas of our lives.

How do we fight him best? How do we avoid falling victim to the land mines he sets on every possible path our lives take?

Stay near unto God. That's the best antidote. The closer we are to the Father, the better our chance of escape. It's that simple. Be near unto God.

REND THE HEAVENS

Oh that thou wouldst rend the heavens,
that thou wouldest come down.
—Isaiah 64:1

After the horror at Golgotha and the glory of the resurrection, Jesus Christ our Savior didn't need to return to this earth. But he did. With his crucified and resurrected body, he wasn't a citizen of the world at all, yet he stayed. Hanging around here below was something unnatural for him, yet he appeared, time and time again, to his disciples.

One possible reason is love. He loved his disciples so much that he couldn't, perhaps, leave them with the pictures they must have carried in their memories—Peter at the courtroom, John at the foot of the cross beneath a horridly darkened sky. He had to come again to reassure them and to buttress their faith.

But his extraordinary forty-day visit had to end. And it did. That last perfect moment on the Mount of Olives—with Gethsemane at its foot, with Jerusalem spread beautifully behind it, with Golgotha and the tomb from which he'd risen behind—must have seemed, to his disciples, a sublime panorama, a divine canvas that suggested bits of every hour of his short stay among them. Then he arose. He disappeared miraculously behind the clouds. But even as he did, the angels appeared, offering comfort. "He is gone from you, but one day to return," they explained. "One day the whole world shall be his."

Where exactly did Jesus Christ go that day? We're told he ascended, but to what place? A whole region above the clouds? The fact is, we really don't know.

Natural voices within us tell us that the direction is not down, but up. We're told the earth is God's footstool, after all, and we look up for light—for the sun, the moon, and the stars. Rains fall from heaven to nurture the earth. But we have no proof that somewhere, miles and miles and miles into the ionosphere, there is a city of gold.

We know very well that physical dimensions mean absolutely nothing to God Almighty. And all of us know that the heavens aren't hewn out of pink granite or poured from concrete trucks. Even a child believes that God's holy temple isn't built out of ponderosa pine or bird's-eye maple. Those kinds of materials simply aren't divine. Someday—count on it!—we'll know heaven's zip code. But when we discover it, we'll undoubtedly be surprised.

"Oh, that thou wouldst rend the heavens!" says Isaiah (64:1), pitched in worry and sadness. What the prophet feels is his own aspiration blocked by the blackened earth. What he wants overwhelmingly is a bit of the divine. Don't we all.

What he received—what all of us now have—is Jesus Christ. Christ descended from that mysterious realm and then ascended once again. But when he left us behind, he didn't leave us alone. He is, after all, our Head. We continue to live in his light and love, and in turn we continue to bring our faith, love, and hope to his throne. He isn't *not* with us.

In fact, by ascending he hasn't so much increased his distance from us, but rather come even closer. No more do we have to hope for some phantom-like appearance in an upper room or on a mountain in Galilee. He's all over today, all around, the very ruler of those regions with which Satan tempted him, regions he took as his own with the blessing of the Father. By Christ, the heavens have been torn open to us, never to be closed again.

To believe that fully—to know him— is to taste of divine and heavenly glory. The soul that is cherished by the blessed glow of light, love, and life already participates with the divine. Those who in this life have come near unto God, with great joy watch the hour approach when they too shall enter final glory. That very same comfort and confidence enabled early Christians to carry off the bodies of their martyred friends with songs of jubilation.

We live, today, in a whole different era. But we have the very same assurance those early Christians did, because this God, this Jesus Christ, this heaven-opener, is ours. Because of him, this much we know: heaven is ours, now and forever.

WITH ALL THE SAINTS

That ye, being rooted and grounded in love, may be able to comprehend with all saints what is the breadth, and length, and depth, and height; and to know the love of Christ, which passeth knowledge, that ye might be filled with all the fulness of God.
—*Ephesians 3:17-19*

I t may seem ogre-like for someone to criticize another believer for saying, as so many do today, that Jesus Christ is his or her "personal savior." Upbraiding someone for such a common, pious expression may even seem sinful. But be careful if you speak of God in that way—not because the words are wrong, but because appropriating the King of the universe in that singular fashion risks dwarfing God's very character.

Although the language of the Lord's Prayer is third-person—*our* Father who art in heaven"; "forgive *us* our debts as *we* forgive our debtors"—we certainly may and do convert that into the first person when we address God in our prayers. On the other hand, we suffer when our prayers are laced with personal references.

Just think about it. Even though our sins are mostly personal, the fact remains that all our sins and miseries flow from a common source. We've all rejected him, no matter what the genre of our particular offense. As a result, we all need his grace, which comes, of course, from a single source—God Almighty. We're different, but very, very much alike.

Is our praise personal? Not really. Since God extends to all of us his grace, all of us thank him for an identical blessing. Besides, Satan wrestles with all of us, and when, through grace, we defeat him, we all thank the same Divine Goodness.

Together believers stand before God. Notice how inclusive the apostle is: "with all the saints," he says. Many of us know other believers in our churches and communities, and we appreciate their friendship and fellowship. But don't ever forget that a multitude of believers live, breathe, and worship all over the globe. Tons of saints have come before us; millions will follow, as long as the Lord tarries. We, together, are "all the saints."

But there's more to this. We don't even know how many believers are around us at any one time. We tend to judge others in ways that God doesn't. On the other hand, people are not redeemed by our thinking that they are. God redeems; his choice is what counts. It's altogether possible, given our own weakness, that the number of believers existing at any one time is much larger than the number our discriminating minds would count.

Think of how narrow your horizons are when you assume that only your friends, your church people, or those from your theological heritage comprise "all the saints." The rest of the world is, by that view, little more than a mess—and the fact is, it isn't.

Now try to picture "all the saints," the whole body of Christ; it's more vast than any rock concert or protest group, a far bigger crowd than the Million Man March. And you're part of it. You're one with them, Christ as your head. All of those people have struggled through life—many of them more painfully than you. Our souls soar when we think about this. No computer can tally the number. Only God does this census.

Consider this. We're brothers and sisters to Paul, to Samson, to Rahab, to Joseph, to the disciples, and to Mary, mother of Christ. We are. We're all one body. Incredible. God's heart is so big that only our own heart's smallness can keep us away.

Talk of him as your personal Savior, come to him alone and in thanksgiving, but never measure him by the standards of your own personality. To do that is to mistake his immensity for our own diminutive natures. Understand the vast extent of his cosmic brother- and sisterhood, know you're a part of it, and your understanding of God grows exponentially.

The nearer you come to understand the huge tent of his grace, the nearer you come to knowing him face to face. We're all part of his immense holy bundle of believers. The Lord God Almighty is your personal God, and ever so much more.

THE GRACE OF
OUR LORD

The grace of the Lord Jesus Christ, and the love of God,
and the communion of the Holy Ghost, be with you all. Amen.
—2 Corinthians 13:14

Of all the benedictions Paul uses in his letters, the final prayer/blessing of 2 Corinthians is the one that stuck, the one that has been sounded for thousands of years from pulpits all over Christendom: "The grace of our Lord Jesus Christ, and the love of God, and the communion of the Holy Spirit, be with you all." How many millions of times hasn't that line placed perfectly wonderful end punctuation on Christian worship?

Some would say, "too often." In worship as in life, when repetition becomes mindless, something has to be done. But those who insist that repetition is always mindless, forget, rather mindlessly, that sometimes the problem lies in the mind, not in the repetition.

Paul's benediction is a blessing, and blessing is an act we don't do much of anymore. Christ blessed the disciples after his resurrection; "Peace be with you," he said. Old Jacob, deceived as he was, still wanted to bless his children at the end of his life.

Does anyone ever do that anymore? Have you heard of old men or women on their deathbeds imparting blessings to the family? For the most part, all we talk about today is whether our loved ones' last moments were fitful or easy.

And there's a flip side here, a biblical tradition of cursing that's vanished as completely as blessing. We're not talking about the strings of expletives one hears on the street and in the media today, generated by meanness, anger, or hatred. What we're referring to is justified cursing, inspired from above and spoken with God's own authority.

Let's face it, both blessing and cursing have fallen on hard times. The only cursing heard today is, well, you've heard it or seen it scribbled on walls. And blessing has dissolved into insipid little ditties like "Have a nice day" or a yellow smiley face sticker.

Only in the church has any kind of traditional blessing lived on. Sometimes people kneel, sometimes they merely bow their heads, often they repeat "Amen" to conclude Paul's benediction to the Corinthians. But that those words live on is a wonderful thing.

Why? Because they remind us that we're not creatures of this world only. As believers depart worship, Paul's benediction urges us to remember that the church of the living God stands in touch with a higher order of reality than the world itself offers. It tells us our Divine Governor isn't the president or the prime minister.

All believers live in two worlds—the one they inhabit with the saints and the one they occupy with unbelievers. Actually, those two worlds dovetail. Grace and peace and love have affected life in this world, brought justice and mercy, respect and dignity, and freedom. But the actual merging of the grace, peace, and fellowship of God with this world occurs only in believers who, while they live in this world, carry the higher order of God in their hearts, a higher order coming from intimate fellowship with God Almighty.

Those who walk with God know there are two worlds and feel it most acutely in fellowship with others. In the company of the world, a whole different tone exists, a different language, different meanings for words like *love*. In the company of the world, believers often feel difficulty opening the flower of their inner lives.

For that reason, some run away from the world; but that's not the right thing to do. We have a calling from God; there's work to be done. Besides, the last thing we want to present is an image that others see as spiritual pride. We can't fall victim to their thinking that we're better. And we certainly better not think it ourselves. Our first calling is no less real than Christ's—*to* this world, not *away* from it.

And that's why, as we leave worship, we need to hear that our real fellowship is the grace of Christ, the love of God, and the communion of the Holy Spirit. That's why it's important that this blessing be cherished, repeated time and time again. It is an assurance that the triune God will be ours because—and this is grace!—he wants to be close to us.

I Am a Jealous God

Thou shalt not bow down thyself to them, nor serve them: for I the LORD thy God am a jealous God, visiting the iniquity of the fathers upon the children unto the third and fourth generation of them that hate me.
—Exodus 20:5

In one of the tombs at Syracuse, the tyrant Dionysius once managed to affect an incredible echo with the express purpose of listening to every word muttered by those he imprisoned there. Even today, at that spot one can hear the rustling of paper several hundred feet away. Because the prisoners knew he was listening, however, they watched every last word they said. His presence dominated their spirit and their existence.

Our God once said this to his prophet Ezekiel: "Thus have you said, O house of Israel, for I know the things that come into your mind, every one of them. Thus also what ought, but does not come into it" (translation from the Dutch version). Believers, it seems, should be just as conscious of the Lord as Dionysius's prisoners were of him. And more so. After all, the Creator of heaven and earth knows not only what we say aloud, but what never escapes our lips but exists in our thoughts anyway. He reads carefully even the impulses that never make it into our words.

If you don't believe that, then God's power doesn't course through you. If you act as if that isn't true, you really don't believe in God.

So how should this truth affect us? With fear, obviously. From the break of dawn to the moment we fall asleep—and then some—we need to be on-line with the Father. We need to avoid hateful speech, rancorous thoughts, unholy impulses. We need to reign in our darkness. He's there, after all, always.

But is *fear* the prime motivation of the believer's life? No. Fear's opposite is, actually: love. Think about it. Our most blessed privilege as believers is being near to him. Like nothing else, we enjoy his nearness and fellowship, his presence in our lives.

But our nearness is his joy too. Because we are God's children, he loves our fellowship. He made us, after all. We're stamped with his image. And that's why he feels hurt when we leave him, when we don't obey him or keep him in our thoughts. When he gets left behind, he grieves. In fact, throughout Scripture he uses imagery drawn from our most intimate relationships to make his pain vivid.

When we love someone, we can't abide separation. We're bothered by our spouses' attentions going anywhere other than ourselves. We get jealous, very jealous.

God has, in a way, married us. We are Christ's bride, his church. That's the language of Scripture. And just as a spouse suffers profoundly from any kind of alienation, God suffers our wandering souls with great distress, even jealousy.

So being near unto God has its own perverse backside. Those who aren't near to him incur his wrath for giving their hearts elsewhere. And the fact is, there isn't a lot of space to work with here: if we don't give our hearts to God, we give them elsewhere—to our work, our play, or another.

One more thing. In marriage, sometimes what we think—and even what we do—never really gets known by our spouses. Not so with God. There's no play-acting, no fake smiles, no false kisses. He knows absolutely everything. And he wants it all.

Is it too much to ask that we be conscious of him? Is it too much to ask that our hearts seek his face? Is it too much to ask that he be considered every day of our lives?

In avoiding his jealousy, our lives are cherished and blessed. He's the source of love, after all, and all our ability to love others—family, spouse, country—stems from our love for him and his love for us.

If he didn't love us *all the time*, his jealousy wouldn't be so profound. But he does. God Almighty doesn't play around. His love is more constant than ours will ever be.

The triune God cannot and will not abide our adultery. He wants us fully, as he loves us and as he has given himself for us. In a way, knowing the extent of his love makes our coming to him easier, doesn't it?

THE SIGNS
OF THE TIMES

Ye can discern the face of the sky;
but can ye not discern the signs of the times?
—Matthew 16:3

Those whose livelihood is dependent upon the weather learn quickly how to read the sky. Sailors can rattle off a dozen quips and verses, remnant wisdom of years of experience: "Red in the morning, sailors take warning; red at night, sailor's delight."

When Christ himself talks about the "signs of the times," however, he is not talking about something as regular and readable as blazing horizons. The skies, after all, looked the same to Abraham as they do to us. The signs of the times, however, are always different, always changing. Old quips rarely work.

Example? During the Reformation, religion was on everyone's mind. In the pulpit, the courtroom, the market, and at the family dinner table, religion was often used as the decision-maker. If religion were water vapor in an evening sky, every nightfall would have been brilliantly red during Luther's time.

But religiosity dissipated in the eighteenth century; the red glow became nonexistent. Faith withdrew, and in public life, religion was debased to silly quarreling, self-conceit, laughter, and scorn. In the nineteenth century, culture returned to a higher seriousness, but science took the throne proudly, served in its court by modernist theology, skepticism, and cold unbelief.

Spirituality seems to have been reborn in the twentieth century. Culture seems more receptive to mystical religious feeling, to spiritism, and to anything Eastern; but there's no return to the Man of Sorrows. People want religion, but not Christianity.

Some Christians, in a Pharisee-like way, don't care about these changes. They're happy enough with their hard-and-fast rules: if they don't do certain things, they feel they're following God's ways exactly. Platitudes rule.

But true disciples of Christ watch the sky, read the lay of the land, and know something about the culture in which they live because they understand that spirituality and culture are not mutually exclusive. They know it because they recognize that the culture in which they live affects them daily, hourly; and they want to know how and why. What they also know deeply is that holding their ground means not letting go of the cross.

In the middle of an unsympathetic culture, faith is an oasis, a place where one can drink deeply of meaning and love. But believers cannot think themselves privileged, for no believers made it to the oasis on their own. By grace alone we've come to peace.

In culture today, to stay near unto God demands tenacity. We climb with hands and feet, and if we get to the top of the mountain, often there's still a fog. Holding fast is a battle. But it's a battle worth fighting. When we hold on by grace, we may well savor a greater peace than believers in other eras; once you know the dread of storms, calm seas and bright, sparkling skies are more beautiful than ever.

But having found peace, we know very well the threat to those still in danger. We know how tough it is out there. We want more of the millions in the wilderness to know the peace of the oasis. We can't help being concerned for their eternal welfare.

So don't hide your faith. Don't keep your mouth shut. Don't call your cowardice *toleration* or *respect*. And don't hold yourself aloof. Take part in life. Be at home in this world—it's still his. Know what is of interest and beauty in culture. Keep the terrain of this world in front of you so you can discover what motivates those who still haven't found their home in the Lord. Witness to peace with love, not argument. When you suffer ridicule, as you will, walk away; but don't forget that in the throes of his greatest suffering, Christ prayed urgently for those who brought him there.

If what remains foremost in our minds are those imperiled by a culture that's sworn allegiance to a force other than the I AM, as God's people we will, in our daily lives, be ever near unto him who has brought us to love itself.

WHEN I WAS A CHILD

When I was a child, I spake as a child, I understood as a child,
I thought as a child: but when I became a man,
I put away childish things.
—1 Corinthians 13:11

Good manners are important, but they play a significant role only in our most formal relationships. Friendship, like love, doffs conventionality quickly. A formal handshake, polite nods, and winning smiles are the stuff of formal relationships. Wherever intimacy grows, the baggage gets tossed in a moment. We don't necessarily dispense with good manners in our closest friendships, but the conventions of polite address are as nonessential to real friendship as a thickly starched shirt.

And that's the way it is with our relationship to God. Our own hidden fellowship doesn't wear the trappings of what "is expected" by others. We don't imitate others. If we do, our relationship becomes mechanical—and being near unto God absolutely cannot be mechanical. Form kills. Imitation delivers nothing. What's real in our relationship to God grows out of our own experience.

Think about it. Being near unto God is different for all of us. Gender has something to do with how we approach him; so does economic background. Our dispositions, our personality types, our physical conditions, all these characteristics affect the way we walk with God. Sisters, born and reared in the very same household, have different ways of building fellowship with the Father. We're all a little bit different. Why should our fellowship be the same? Uniformity in all intimate relationships is death.

Run through your own life for a minute here. Those times when you felt yourself closest to God could have been in moments of anguish, triumph, joy, deep sorrow, or regret. There's nothing standard here, no recommended procedure, no set of instructions. Just as married couples celebrating golden anniversaries will be the first to say that the colors of love change like a vivid sunset over the years, we all know our closest and dearest walk with God changes from the playhouse to the retirement home.

The apostle knew it. "When I was a child, I spake as a child, I understood as a child, I thought as a child," he writes, "but when I became a man, I put away childish things" (1 Cor. 13:11).

Children have something of an instinct for spiritual life. They love fables and fairy tales; many have a belief in ghosts and goblins that gives them a dread of darkness so that parents have to leave the light on and check under the bed. They seem fascinated by the reality of a spiritual world.

Children who can't read the Bible or understand a page of catechism can be almost ravished by their personal sense of God. Extremely impressionable, their inner lives are governed almost totally by what we might call instinct.

These characteristics are God-designed. The natural piety of a child creates an intimacy that's a blessing to behold. It's a joy to teach a child to pray. What Christ had in mind when he talked about a childlike faith was a quality of inspiration and wonder left unclouded by the anxiety of our adult doubt, a quality of inspiration that is childlike.

Given all of this, our handling of our children's faith is critical. Whenever parents or teachers seek to make kids into miniature adults, kids lose. It's painful to observe parents teaching their kids the mechanics of faith, as if intimacy was technologically acquired.

But it's just as wrong to leave them alone, to assume that somehow kids will simply grow into faith the way they grow into work clothes. A child's heart responds to God almost instinctively. Not to nurture that heart in faith is to prompt suffering throughout adulthood.

In time, children need to learn the creeds, the history of the church, the history of revelation itself. In time, children grow into adults. But there will no adult intimacy if kids aren't allowed to seek fellowship with God in their own ways, on their own time. That's the nature of things.

MAKE ABODE
WITH THEE

Jesus answered and said unto him, If a man love me, he will
keep my words: and my Father will love him, and we will
come unto him, and make our abode with him.
—John 14:23

Who doesn't feel the excitement of Christmas each year, when Bethlehem's manger is celebrated all over the world? Who can't be inspired by the old Luke 2 story? Who can't be thrilled on Christmas Eve? Few, very few. Dickens created one of literature's most enduring characters by giving him a line vehemently contrary to what we all recognize as the spirit of the season. Scrooge has to say "Bah! Humbug!" but once, and every reader knows his problem.

But if we stay at Bethlehem, if we center our sense of God's own identity on the Word made flesh, we miss the entirety of the gospel's triumphant joy. For while the apostles' own fervor was ignited by their having known Christ, having seen him and touched him, there's more to God's love than the story of God's Son sent to earth.

There is, for instance, the entire Old Testament. Even though Jesus is not sent into this world at the very beginning of time, the story of God's love begins long before Mary's travail in a barn. The gospel was already proclaimed in Paradise, as New Testament writers attest in countless allusions to the Old. The truths of the New Covenant were planted in the ancient texts as seeds that would blossom in the reality of Jesus Christ.

The law given to Moses isn't simply the Ten Commandments. What we refer to as Moses' law includes the whole book of instruction for life, the revelation of God delivered to Israel, God's Word. What was already there in outline form became eternally filled in with Christ's birth and death and resurrection. Undoubtedly, we see the reality of love most clearly in the Word made flesh, but the shape of that love was revealed long before.

Think for a minute about the word *dwell*. To dwell does not mean "to visit." We know that God dwells in heaven; Christ told us as much. But heaven and earth are not altogether separate, because we know very well that God dwells in us as well.

Here's the whole story. God lived in Paradise. When Adam sinned, God left but didn't abandon his people. "Adam, where art thou?" he asked, searching. He came back, time and time again. He *dwells*.

In Israel, God *lived* at Zion. That was the divine address. For a while, God appeared as a cloud, then as a column of fire. He was there, dwelling among them. "This is my habitation," said the Lord. "This is my holy place."

At Bethlehem, the great restoration occurred because Immanuel graced our lives with his presence. God came back and *dwelt* among us. But even when Jesus ascended, he didn't really leave. In fact, God came back as if broadcast. No longer was he limited to a certain place (Israel) or a certain people (only those who saw him).

Only when Jesus was no longer seen and heard on this earth could he be exalted and glorified on the throne of grace, because only then could he offer his Spirit to every people on every continent in every age. That's why Christ himself explains the necessity of his leaving: "I shall come again, and with the Father make my abode with you." He not only was forecast to be with us in the Old Testament, he was with us in the New; and now he *is* with us.

Even the saints tend to push him out of their lives; even the best of us want to relegate God to the corners of our existence, to marginalize him. Sin, whether it occurs in Paradise or Parkersburg, always tries to expel God.

But here's the beauty of the full blossoming gospel: he returns, time and time again. He won't let us get away. He loves us so much that he keeps coming back.

To have the Spirit is to have God in one's own heart and soul. The new commandment of love for others is based in the recognition that human beings carry something eternal, something of God—that they carry, in fact, God. We are called to love others because he lives in them—that's why. This is the gospel for all time. It's not just sweet Christmas music, but a gospel that leaps out of the manger and lives in us. That's the miraculous good news.

That's the reason to thank God with our lives.

WHOM HAVE I IN HEAVEN BUT THEE?

Whom have I in heaven but thee? and there is
none upon earth that I desire beside thee.
—Psalm 73:25

A kind of special grace comes to all of us in calm and beautiful deathbed testimonies. Perhaps those who stand right at the threshold of eternity, who glimpse what is to be seen of glory without quite stepping over, know better than any of us the matchless wonder of God's love. When the dying testify to what they see, we are all blessed—and God is honored.

No one should ever believe that those who don't have beautific visions on their deathbeds haven't lived righteous lives. Sickness robs some of the best believers in the world of the quiet sensibility necessary to see and communicate the joy that awaits us at God's throne. Some people are simply high-strung, nervous. Sometimes the dying are too young to want to go easily. Often, a coma or some other wretched malady keeps people from communicating anything at all at their demise.

Oddly enough, God has granted some of the world's great scoundrels a beautiful death, a moment when his glory seemed an arm's reach away—and it was. On the other hand, wonderful, saintly people have fought pain and anguish to the moment of release. Remember, not all the Old Testament saints saw glory as gloriously as Jacob did.

But what's most touching about deathbed testimonies is their remarkable purity. More people fake piety than arc pious. Faking it is easy, and we all do it, trying to literally look good. But deathbeds jettison pretense. No one acts when they face the grave. There's no reason to build character or reputation. Nothing is left in this world.

And that's what Asaph sees in Psalm 73. When he anticipates glory, he lets all the baggage of life go and testifies to this singular truth: there is nothing in heaven but God Almighty. What he says is a perfect testimony, isn't it?

God gives us so much to love in life that we can hardly find room for it all. There are spouses, of course, and family. There are friends and neighbors. There are rainbows and hummingbirds and skies full of sun. We love our work—and we should. Each of us carries more investments than the most well-heeled Wall Street broker because we have so much to love here below. It's well we should. People who try not to love, live unnaturally.

But in heaven there's nothing but God. That's Asaph's testimony: "Who have I in heaven but thee?" Nobody else. Nothing at all. Only the Lord.

The holy art of living as a child of God is to love things of this world to such an extent that we see everything as gifts from the King of Glory. We give our hearts away on earth to a host of inclinations and callings after visible things, but we see the beauty of all that we love in most vivid detail when we see all of it as blessing, as the Lord's.

But why see the text as a kind of deathbed testimony only? It isn't. Try this test on yourself. If you had nothing on your back or in your cupboards or anywhere around you, if you had absolutely nothing aside from God, would you be complete?

That question is at the heart of things. After all, sometimes we love God for his ability to complete our happiness. When we ask him for things, even for favors, we appear to want to use him, as if he were a philanthropist or a game-show host. That's not at issue here. He alone is at issue. If you seek him to help you out, you're not seeking him, but his aid.

Imagine your own deathbed—that seems morbid in today's world, but it's a good practice. Think of yourself dying. If at that moment—and now—you can be thrilled with the knowledge that what awaits you in glory is absolutely nothing but God, if that idea can shake you, move you, make you weep, then you're blessed. Believe me, you are. Then you are, right now, near unto God. ❖

AS THE HART PANTETH AFTER THE WATER BROOKS

Psalm 42

Few poems in the history of literature are as powerfully written as Psalm 42, perhaps because few poems so achingly convey the desperation one feels when apart from the Source of comfort and strength in our lives. Even though no experience is so wonderful as being near unto God, our souls still regularly turn toward dozens of the world's neon distractions. Even so, we know very well we've wandered and where we really want to be, and for that reason we can be absolutely driven to find the meaning and truth that we know only when we are near to God.

We're strange creatures, so messed up. We come to him, of course, in a variety of ways. Sickness and danger often drive us to our knees. Loneliness imperils our souls. At times, we're wounded by the assault of somebody in our circles; we feel beaten. Sometimes life itself seems a losing cause, and we're thrown back on God, our refuge and our strength.

But the passion of Psalm 42 does not arise out of suffering, but out of simple need. No war or sadness or sickness prompts the psalmist to this testimony; it's not conscience or some angelic siren song that draws him to God. What arises in his heart comes only from the urgency of his own spiritual instinct, his—and our—deep need for God.

Dehydration cannot be taken lightly. People die from lack of water more quickly and frequently than from lack of food. If we think of *thirst* as something remedied by a cold can of pop, we're missing the force of this poem. A deer, a buck, has been wandering through the woods all day in search of a brook. When he arrives at its bank, he finds nothing but dry creek bed. Now an animal doesn't think, doesn't process his *angst* or try to find himself. What this buck does is simply raise his head and punish his own parched throat with a piercing scream that echoes off the trees. Such is his urgency.

Ask yourself this: how often have you simply longed for God? Don't count those times when grief or sadness or worry kept you anxious; that's not what this psalm is about. How often have we truly desired, for God's sake, to be near to him? Piety simply doesn't make it here—it's self-inflated pretense. How often do we authentically thirst for God?

That we want him is proof of his nature in us, a mark of our divinity. But that we don't pursue him is a mark of our sin. We'll find no rest outside of his presence. We know that, yet we have this horrible habit of looking for him in all the wrong places.

No creed will satisfy, no nicely formulated idea about God, no relic or symbol. What we need is the living water—and not brakish, swampy stuff either. We need water that tumbles and leaps and rushes, water that is alive.

The psalmist looks for God in his sanctuary at Zion, but then the psalmist was an Israelite. We aren't. We live in a different time. And if we think that we can simply analogize Zion to the church sanctuary, we're wrong. God is in our churches, but he's also in our homes and our workplaces. The thirst for comfort and meaning in life is in the heart, not in the church. Zion isn't a bedroom corner where you pray, it isn't the church sanctuary, and it isn't a circle of intimate friends.

Our being near unto God isn't limited by time and space. It's not something that happens only inside stained-glass windows. Zion is a sidewalk, an office, a kitchen, a classroom, a factory, a library carrel. Zion is where we come to God through Christ. That's where we find our thirst finally relieved by living water. Zion is Christ really, our Mediator and our King, who is himself God, to whom be glory for ever and ever. Amen!

When we are redeemed, we are in Christ and Christ is in us. We are woven wonderfully as living members into the mystical body of Christ, our natures melted together into his divinity in the most intimate way.

What a Savior! What a God! We can be near unto him at any time, any place, in any circumstance, because he is always near to us. Hallelujah!